L.I.F.E. Guide for Spouses

A Workbook for Living in Freedom Everyday

in Sexual Wholeness and Integrity

Melissa Haas

with core material by
Mark Laaser

Edited by Debbie and Mark Laaser, Ph. D.
L.I.F.E. Guides for Living in Freedom Everyday

L.I.F.E. *Guide* for Spouses
by Melissa Haas

Printed in the United States of America

ISBN 978-0-9816796-19

NOTE: This workbook is not intended to provide therapy, counseling, clinical advice or treatment, or to take the place of clinical advice and treatment from a professional mental health provider or personal physician. Readers are advised to consult qualified healthcare providers regarding mental, emotional and medical issues. Neither the publisher, the author, nor L.I.F.E. Ministries assumes any responsibility for any possible consequences from any reader's action or application of information in this workbook.

Color House Graphics
www.colorhousegraphics.com

Foreword
from L.I.F.E. Ministries

Sexual dysfunction has become a common cancer within today's culture, and the church is certainly not exempt. The number of people struggling with sexual brokenness has sky-rocketed due to two main factors: the prevalence and availability of pornography and a sexually saturated media. Mark Laaser has commented that our entire society is being sexually abused by this onslaught. Unhealthy and unscriptural sexual behaviors such as pornography, compulsive masturbation, and adultery are just as prevalent within the Christian community as they are in the society at large. Among believers, there are men and women—including key leaders—who, because of painful experiences and sinful choices, compulsively use sex and unholy relationships as an escape or medication to help them cope with life. The consequences of these behaviors are devastating to the strugglers and also to their family and friends.

Many of those who struggle with life-dominating sexual behaviors desperately long to be free from their bondage and intensely desire to live in sexual integrity They want to experience genuine L.I.F.E.—Living in Freedom Everyday. The *L.I.F.E. Guide for Men* and the *L.I.F.E. Guide for Women* were written to help God's people be free from the bondage of sexual addiction and to equip them to walk in His unconditional love and defining truth. L.I.F.E. Ministries is grateful to have Dr. Mark Laaser, an internationally known author and leader in the area of sexual addiction recovery, as the author of the *L.I.F.E. Guide for Men* and the general editor of the *L.I.F.E. Guide* series. Dr. Laaser conceptualized the Seven Principles on which each workbook is based. A respected expert in a specific area of ministry—women, adolescents, spouses—adapted the material for that target population. This design provides consistency of information and terminology throughout the *L.I.F.E. Guide* series.

This *L.I.F.E. Guide for Spouses* is the fourth in the *L.I.F.E. Guide* series. It is dedicated to helping spouses grieve the losses associated with their mate's sexual addiction, walk in freedom from the bondage of codependence, and grow in God's unconditional love and defining truth as they take the healing journey of transformation.

The L.I.F.E. Ministries support group program offers Christ-centered and relationally oriented groups that incorporate spiritual discipline, small group accountability, and ongoing prayer and support for those struggling with sexual brokenness and their spouses. L.I.F.E. Groups are support groups, not therapy groups. While there is much within each of the *L.I.F.E. Guides* and the recommended recovery materials to help participants identify and deal with the wounds from the past, we also encourage individual therapy to address root issues that often lead to sexual addiction and co-addiction. Healing this core woundedness is vital to living in freedom everyday, and most people need the help of a trained counselor.

The ongoing support so critical to the process of transformation comes from the networking of lives through L.I.F.E. Groups. These groups involve real relationships—open, transparent, and accountable connections with fellow participants. L.I.F.E. Groups value confidentiality and maintain an absolute commitment to provide a safe atmosphere for complete honesty and complete acceptance, where members are embraced in an attitude of love and forgiveness by others sharing common hurts and struggles. All of these components guide the group members toward Christ-centered transformation, according to the conviction that our true identity and the way we live it out are found in the freedom and grace that only Jesus can offer.

Registration with L.I.F.E Ministries

We encourage all groups using this L.I.F.E. Guide workbook to become registered L.I.F.E. Groups. Registering your L.I.F.E. Group with L.I.F.E. Ministries International entitles your group leadership to access additional information and discounted resources and opens additional communication links for information about conferences, workshops, and leadership training—often at substantial discounts. Through newsletters and the L.I.F.E. Ministries website, your group leaders will have access to materials and information to help your L.I.F.E. Group grow and to expand your sexual addiction ministry within your church and your community. Your group will also be listed in our network of L.I.F.E. Groups and other sexual addiction ministries, so those looking for help in your community can find it, and your group members will never be without needed support when away from home. Finally, by registering, your group will be furthering the work of L.I.F.E. Ministries International and will help make this support group ministry available in additional churches and communities across the country and around the world.

To find out more information, to start a L.I.F.E. Group, or to register your L.I.F.E. Group, check out the ministry's website, call L.I.F.E. Ministries toll-free, or write for more information. We would love to welcome you and start you on the journey toward Living in Freedom Everyday in His unconditional love.

L.I.F.E. Ministries International
P.O. Box 952317
Lake Mary, FL 32795

866-408-LIFE (866-408-5433)

www.freedomeveryday.org

Foreword
By Mark Laaser, Ph.D.

There is a proverbial saying, "If I had a dollar for every…" Most of the time when we use it, we are exaggerating. In the case of this workbook, however, if I had a dollar for every time I'm asked about when is there going to be a resource for the spouses of sex addicts, I really would be a rich man.

It is surprising to me that at this time in our field there really hasn't been a good resource. There have been those who have tried, but it seems to me that the books that have come out are full of trite, black and white, incorrect, and (at times) abusive teaching. Wives have been told to:

-Forgive and forget.
-It may have been your fault. If only you had been more sexual.
-Your husband's emotional needs can only be opened up sexually.
-Remember, it is your biblical responsibility to submit.
-There really is no hope, you should just get divorced.

One book, in a popular recent series, makes it sounds like husbands will literally explode if their wives don't have sex with them enough.

Finally, however, we have a book of rich substance, sound advice, and (most importantly) hope. Melissa Haas has truly written a powerful resource that will help thousands. First, Melissa is a good writer. This book is easy to read and understand. Next, it is sound clinically and leads spouses through the process of growth and change. She knows about this through her own journey and through her work with many spouses in Atlanta. Finally, and most foundationally, this book is sound scripturally and is an outstanding source of biblical wisdom.

More than all of these factors, the power of this book is that it is written from the heart. Only those who have made a painful journey can write so profoundly about it. From the shock of discovery and the despair of wondering how to keep a family together to the long days and nights of personal and couple's growth, Melissa knows what she is writing about. Such a wife is a treasure of grace and wisdom.

I know about such wives, because I am married to one. If it had not been for Deb, I wouldn't be writing this forward, or anything else for that matter. Deb and I both celebrate what Melissa has done in these pages. We have witnessed the power of transformation that she and her husband Troy have experienced. They are an inspiring couple and doing great work in their ministry together.

We all pray that this workbook will be a blessing to all of you.

Author's Acknowledgements

God's plans for my life always amaze me. Six years ago I was sitting in a dirt-floor hut in northern Kenya trying desperately to be the missionary God had called me to be and wondering if there was any hope for my dying marriage. At the time I didn't know why life was so painful; I just knew that if anything was going to change, God would have to do the changing… and He did. So, my first acknowledgement is to the Faithful One in my life I call Lord. It is His transforming grace in my life that has made it possible for me to experience a life of freedom. It is His divine agenda that has given me the opportunity to share my journey with others.

The journey has been made easier for me by the courageous choices of my husband, Troy. I am so grateful for the ways God has grown him and used him in my life. It is my great joy to be married to a man of great vision and passion. I love and respect him greatly. Without Troy's faithful support and administrative gifts, writing this workbook would have been impossible.

My children, Rachel, Aaron, and Jonathan, deserve recognition as well. They have helped me remember that I am a mother first and a writer second. I value their honesty and their love and am thankful for all the times they waited "just a minute," for Mommy to finish a sentence.

I'm thankful for Bob and Johna Hale and their great vision for reaching out to those who struggle with sexual addiction and their loved ones. I am so encouraged by their faithfulness and their spiritual ears.

I also applaud the love and commitment of Mark and Debbie Laaser for this project. More than anything I respect this couple for walking the journey consistently over the past fifteen plus years. Their relationship with God and each other proves that transformation is possible. I'm grateful to have had a part in contributing to this workbook series and most of all for having the chance to get to know their hearts.

Norm is an answer to prayer. Without his courageous authenticity this workbook would lack a male spouse perspective and would be incomplete. I'm grateful for Norm's willingness to share his journey in order to make a difference in the lives of male spouses.

Two colleagues deserve special thanks as well. Marnie Ferree, director of Bethesda Workshop Ministry in Nashville, Tennessee, is a woman I greatly admire and respect. Her input has been invaluable to me, and I feel honored to call her friend. Richard Blankenship, a wonderful counselor in private practice and a staff counselor for Bethesda workshops, has consistently encouraged me during the writing process. Marnie and Richard are responsible for introducing me to the *L.I.F.E. Guide* series and encouraging me to write the *L.I.F.E. Guide for Spouses.* I am humbled by and grateful for their trust.

I also want to recognize Russell Willingham and my fellow journeyers at New Creation Ministries in Fresno, California. It was at NCM that I first discovered the reality and power of spiritual community. My place on the journey today is in large part due to the faithfulness and authenticity of the people at NCM.

My final acknowledgement goes to all the women of Journey—the spouses' group of Walking Free Ministries at First Baptist Church, Woodstock, Georgia. These spouses have shared their deepest hurts with me and their greatest victories. We have prayed for each other, challenged each other, held each other accountable, and learned to be authentic with each other. Most of all we've enjoyed relationship with each other. I want to especially thank the women in my small group who have prayed me through this entire project—Becky, Deborah, Barbara, Karen, Melanie, Sally, Angela, Annette, Debbie, and Mary. Your love blesses me.

Melissa Haas
May, 2005

L.I.F.E. Guide for Spouses

Table of Contents

Introduction

Welcome, friend, to the journey. As a spouse of a man who struggles with sexual addiction, I understand how you may be feeling as you pick up this workbook. The best way to describe how I felt five years ago was *conflicted.* Part of my heart felt tremendous anger towards my husband while the other felt compassion for him. I felt hopeful and hopeless at the same time. There was disbelief that my spouse had betrayed me in this way but also a profound sense of relief that I wasn't crazy, that there really was something wrong. I was confused and hungry for answers. The "why" of it all haunted me. And then there was the overwhelming pain of all the losses.

My prayer for you as you undertake the journey of Living in Freedom Everyday is that you will first find a safe place to grieve all of the losses associated with your spouses' sexual addiction. And then I pray that you will begin to find the answers you are searching for—not for your spouse, but for yourself.

You see, the journey is not about finding a way to convince your spouse to love and cherish you; it's not about making your spouse become faithful and true. The journey is about finding the freedom to live in the grace and truth of God—no matter what choices your spouse makes. It's about being transformed into the woman or man God has always intended you to be for your good and His glory. We have no power over the desires and choices of others, but we can submit ourselves—our desires and choices—to the Faithful One. In Him, we will always have hope, for He has already taken the journey… and made it.

It is our great honor and privilege to walk with you for a time on this journey. Along the way, you will get to know me as well as two other spouses who have been journeying for a while. Debbie Laaser is the wife of Dr. Mark Laaser, author of the *L.I.F.E. Guide for Men* and general editor of the L.I.F.E. Guide series. Debbie and Mark have been on the journey together for over fifteen years. My husband Troy and I are another testimony of God's grace and healing. We've been on the healing journey for five years now, and it is our great joy to walk with other men and women who are struggling as addicts and co-addicts, helping them to experience the life of freedom God wants them to have. The third spouse sharing his story in these pages is Norm. He was married to a female sex addict for seventeen years. Although his wife chose to continue in her addiction and the marriage ended in divorce, Norm has experienced great healing and growth in his own life. We hope his story will encourage the male spouses who choose to use this study on their journey. Debbie, Norm, and I are spouses just like you who have learned to walk with grace and truth in response to our spouses' sexual addiction. And we are glad you have joined us.

Welcome. You are greatly loved and accepted.

Melissa
Debbie
Norm

How to Use this L.I.F.E. Guide

Welcome to the fourth workbook in the L.I.F.E. Guide series written especially for you as a spouse of someone struggling with sexual addiction. Our hope is that you will use this guide in conjunction with a L.I.F.E. Group. ***We believe that relationships are vital to healing and transformation.*** If there is not a L.I.F.E. Group close to you, then consider starting your own. At the very least, as you work through this guide, ask two or three mature believers to support you on the healing journey by meeting with you once a week and listening as your share your assignments with them.

We also want to encourage you to find a professional counselor who understands the dynamics of sexual addiction and co-addiction to walk with you on your journey. While having a counseling relationship is not absolutely vital to recovery, we believe that you will experience healing and change more quickly if you have the opportunity to work individually with a safe professional who can guide you toward truth about yourself and your relationships. There is one word of caution, however. A counselor or pastor who does not understand the dynamics of sexual addiction can be more harmful than helpful. ***Be sure to choose a counselor who has experience dealing with addicts and their spouses.***

Your Private Journal

The first thing you will need to do is to get a journal of some sort. There are many options to choose from—a spiral bound notebook, a fancier bound journal, or a three-ring binder to which you can add pages. Your goal in choosing a journal is to have something that feels comfortable writing in and is easiest for you to use. Although there is space to briefly answer questions in some of the lessons, the leaders of L.I.F.E. Ministries deliberately chose not to put a great deal of writing space in this workbook in order for you to be able to refer back to the material over and over again. Instead, we want you to do the bulk of your writing assignments in your journal. Assignments are clearly marked so that you will easily understand what you are to record in your journal.

Be sure to put your name on your journal. It will become <u>your sacred document</u>, and no one else should see it unless you decide to share it. Remember the old diaries with locks on them? Get that idea in your mind. This is *your* journal for you to record your answers and thoughts with complete honesty. We don't want anyone else reading it uninvited.

Sometimes others may want to look at your journal. Your spouse will probably be one of them. While it is understandable that your spouse wants to know how you are thinking and feeling right now, ***it is a healthy and necessary boundary to keep private the contents of this diary about your life.*** Don't be afraid to set this boundary. (It may be helpful to keep your journal out of plain sight so that others will not be tempted to read it.) The writing that you do in your journal is between you and God. Pray for the power of the Holy Spirit to help you be honest and thorough and to guard your writing from unauthorized eyes.

You may at times want to show what you've written to your counselor, your pastor, others in your small group, or your spouse. That choice is acceptable if you decide it is for *your* benefit. Please don't share what you've written to manipulate or hurt others. Also, refuse to be pressured by others to share your journal. Whether or not you allow others to read what you've written is your choice and your choice alone.

If you have a spouse on the journey of recovery, he/she will be keeping a journal as well. ***Respect the boundary of your spouse's privacy to the same extent you expect your mate to honor yours.*** It is *never* okay to read someone's journal without their invitation and permission. If you have been guilty of violating this boundary in the past, acknowledge your wrongdoing and commit to honor your spouse's boundary of privacy from now on. Remember, you are responsible for being a person of integrity. Disrespecting the boundaries of others reveals a heart ruled by fear. Choose to walk honestly, believing that God sees your hurts and fears and will meet your deepest needs.

Organization of the L.I.F.E. Guide Material

There are four tiers of assignments in this L.I.F.E. Guide. The first tier contains seven lessons on grieving that are to be completed in the order they are written. After you have completed the Grieving Tier, you will begin work on the Seven Principles of L.I.F.E. Each of the Seven Principles is divided into three assignments. You will work through the assignments one tier at time, beginning with assignment one of Principles One through Seven, going on to assignment two of Principles One through Seven, and finishing with assignment three of each of the Principles.

Ideally, you will work through the Time for Grieving with a core group of spouses and go on to join other spouses already working on the Seven Principles. While working on the Seven Principles, each week the group will focus on one of the Principles as the theme of that meeting. Because some spouses may be further along in recovery than you are, you may be working on assignment one of Principle One while others are working on assignments two or three. The goal is to allow for those beginning the journey as well as those further down the road to be able to discuss together the Principle in focus.

L.I.F.E. Groups are always open to new members who are coming for the first time. For spouses, it is most helpful when a newcomer can work through the Time for Grieving lessons with others who are still processing the losses associated with their spouses' betrayal. When the newcomer has had time to grieve, he/she can then join the group working on the Seven Principles. (If your L.I.F.E. Group for Spouses is still developing and two small groups are not possible, it is acceptable for all of the spouses to meet together. What is most important in the healing process is that relationships are built in a safe and spiritual community.)

Working through the Principles

Once you have completed the Time for Grieving Lessons, you will begin working through the Seven Principles for L.I.F.E. Each of the three assignments for the Seven Principles is designed to take you deeper in the work of a Principle. It is important that you complete the assignments in order since the assignments build on each other. Since we want to give you all of the foundation for recovery before you go deeper into the meaning and practice of each Principle, the plan is that you will work on all seven of the first assignments first, then all seven of the second assignments, and finally all seven of the third assignments. On the next page you will find a table to help you stay on track as you work through the L.I.F.E. Guide.

WEEK	A TIME FOR GRIEVING		PAGE	ASSIGNMENT COMPLETE
1	Grieving the Losses		20	
2	Grieving Safely, Part 1		26	
3	Grieving Safely, Part 2		30	
4	Grieving Honestly		34	
5	Grieving When I'm Angry		37	
6	Grieving Deeply		41	
7	Grieving Well		46	
WEEK	**PRINCIPLE**	**ASSIGNMENT**	**PAGE**	**ASSIGNMENT COMPLETE**
8	1	1	57	
9	2	1	67	
10	3	1	79	
11	4	1	92	
12	5	1	105	
13	6	1	120	
14	7	1	135	
WEEK	**PRINCIPLE**	**ASSIGNMENT**	**PAGE**	**ASSIGNMENT COMPLETE**
15	1	2	58	
16	2	2	68	
17	3	2	80	
18	4	2	93	
19	5	2	106	
20	6	2	121	
21	7	2	136	
WEEK	**PRINCIPLE**	**ASSIGNMENT**	**PAGE**	**ASSIGNMENT COMPLETE**
22	1	3	61	
23	2	3	73	
24	3	3	86	
25	4	3	96	
26	5	3	111	
27	6	3	127	
28	7	3	138	

As you can see there are a total of 28 assignments. Although you may set a goal of completing one assignment per week, don't be disappointed if it takes you several weeks to do one assignment. ***More important than working through this guide quickly is working through it thoroughly.*** That means you need to take the time to do each assignment completely, writing out what you are asked to write—not just thinking about your answers in your mind.

Since your L.I.F.E. Group will be discussing a different Principle each week, be prepared to move on to the next Principle, even if you have not fully completed your assignment from the week before. You can always come back to that assignment later, and it is important to stay on task with the group. And don't worry if you can't get everything done in a week. ***All we ask is that you work some each day in your L.I.F.E. Guide***. Remember, recovery is not a race or a competition: it's a transforming way of life. Allow God to individualize your journey. There may be some weeks He wants to focus on one Principle in your life more than another. Give Him the freedom to work in your heart and life without pressuring yourself to finish the work in a set amount of time. This L.I.F.E. Guide is a living, breathing document. You may work through it a number of times in the course of your healing journey. In fact, we hope you will.

If you get stuck on a particular assignment in the guide, we want to challenge you to talk through your struggles with the members of your small group and/or your counselor. Avoid the temptation to skip the exercise or skimp on writing your answers. ***It is at the point of your greatest struggle that you most need to persevere, for the places you are "stuck" are the places God most needs to heal and transform.*** Don't let the enemy rob you of what God has for you by listening to his discouraging lies. Stay accountable and stay focused. Your determination along with authentic relationships with God and others will result in genuine healing and change.

Also, we want to encourage you to use other materials and resources listed on the L.I.F.E. Ministries website to help you on the journey. We have done our best to cover the various aspects of recovery in this workbook, but it is by no means exhaustive. More than anything we want you to be whole, to live in authentic relationships with others, and to have an increasingly intimate relationship with God. Feel free to use other resources to help you accomplish this goal of transformation and healing.

Don't hesitate to call someone at L.I.F.E. Ministries International if you find you don't understand an assignment. You can also ask others in your small group. It may be scary at first, but as you grow you'll become more comfortable with the practice of asking for help.

What to Expect at a L.I.F.E. Group Meeting

Joining a group of unfamiliar people can be a very scary thing to do—especially when you are dealing with your spouse's sexual addiction and your own internal conflicts and struggles. We applaud your courage to take this step of faith, and we want to make your entry into the group as comfortable as possible.

Each L.I.F.E. Group has a character of it own, but there are certain aspects of L.I.F.E. Group meetings that are consistently found in all L.I.F.E. Groups. When you come to a L.I.F.E. Group meeting, you can expect:

- The group leader will introduce himself/herself and open with prayer.
- Group members will introduce themselves.
- Newcomers to the group will be welcomed.
- Group safety guidelines will be read.
- A group member will lead a devotional time that may include music, a reading from the Bible or a devotional book, a personal story, and/or a lesson on one of the Seven Principles.
- An offering will be taken.
- Any business/announcements related to the group will be discussed.
- The large group will divide into small groups for discussion and accountability.
- Group will last for approximately two hours.

As a newcomer, you are not expected to share during small group time, but other group members will be honored if you do. You may feel overwhelmed with emotion when you come to group the first time. We want you to know that it is okay to cry, to express anger, to talk about your fears, and to feel discouraged. As spouses, we have been where you are and understand what you are feeling. And you are completely loved and accepted.

Coming to group and talking about your spouse's struggles with sexual addiction may be incredibly painful. Often when we talk about what has happened and how we are feeling, the truth about our situation becomes very clear—and very real. Sometimes reality is so painful that you will be tempted to stay away from group in order not to face the truth and the anguish it brings to your heart. In those times when you want to isolate in order to avoid dealing with reality, we want to encourage you to call the group leader or a group member and talk about how you are feeling. Stay connected to others and allow them to support you through your pain. We know it is easier to stay in denial, but healing will only come as you face reality and walk through it with God and other safe people.

Note: *If you are currently leading a new L.I.F.E. Group and want to know more about the L.I.F.E. Group Meeting Format, please refer to Appendix A.*

L.I.F.E. Group Safety Guidelines

It is absolutely essential that every L.I.F.E. Group be safe. Safety produces the best environment for honesty and fellowship. All group members are responsible for observing these Safety Guidelines, and if the Guidelines are violated, group members will confront each other in love. If an individual will not observe the Guidelines consistently and refuses to abide by them after being confronted, that individual will be asked to leave the meeting. The well-being of the entire group is more important than any individual member.

1. **It is safe to be honest. We expect all members to tell the truth.**

2. **It is safe to have feelings. All feelings are acceptable to God and to us.**

3. **We give each other feedback as long as it only reflects our own experience, strength, and hope. Therefore, we begin our feedback with "I," and not "you." We do not give advice.**

4. **We do not preach. We may share messages of spiritual strength, hope, and encouragement, but we avoid comments that include words like, "should," "always," and "never." We also avoid expressions such as, "God says..." or "God's will for your life is..." or "God will be angry if..." We respect where others are on their spiritual journey and allow God to meet them in His way and time.**

5. **We do not shame ourselves or others. We do not put down ourselves or anyone else—including our spouses. Instead, we own our anger and express it appropriately, avoiding name calling and using, "I feel...about...because..." statements.**

6. **Although we may talk about how our spouse's behaviors have affected us, we focus on our own healing and transformation. We do not blame others for our choices. We take responsibility for our actions.**

7. **Group time will be divided among those who ask for time to share.**

8. **We abide by the principle of group confidentiality. We do not reveal the identity of other group members or what others have shared in group, even to our spouses. We may share with others what <u>we</u> have shared in group if we choose to do so. However, we must protect the safety of the group by keeping what other group members share in complete confidence.**

Note on the Limitations of Confidentiality: If anyone discloses that a child, disabled person, or elderly person is being harmed, or there is intent to harm, the L.I.F.E. group leader may be required by law to report to the proper authorities. If a group member discloses threats of harm to self or to others, the law may require that action be taken to protect the parties involved. **It is incumbent on the L.I.F.E. group leader to confirm what the laws are in the state in which the group is meeting, as these may vary.** Some states may require that a group leader also file reports with proper authorities about illegal possession, production, or distribution of child pornography or other types of illegal activities. **We are very clear about these exceptions to confidentiality.**

How to Get the Most Out of L.I.F.E.

The journey of recovery and transformation is a process—not an event. Although healing will take place in your heart and life in God's time, there are things you can do to promote your healing process and progress on the journey. Here are some of them.

- **Attend group meetings consistently.** Authentic relationships grow when people spend time with each other consistently.

- **Do your homework.** We know there will be some weeks you are unable to finish assignments completely. We know you have responsibilities outside of group, and we recognize the importance of family time and other priorities you have in your life. However, in order to grow, you must invest time in your recovery. That means you must be intentional about spending time to work on your assignments. Start by giving God and yourself fifteen minutes each day to address your heart. If you miss a day, that's okay, but try to work as consistently as you can.

- **Allow others to know the real you.** Be honest about your feelings and your behaviors. Risk exposing the things about you and your life of which you are most ashamed. Let God heal any shame you are carrying through the love and acceptance He extends through other group members. Enjoy being in your own skin and taking off pretentious masks that hide the real you.

- **Accept others with no agenda to fix or change them.** Be patient with other group members as God works in their lives. If conflict arises between you and another group member, face it honestly, owning your feelings. Avoid pressuring others to do what you think is best. Support other group members by praying for them and walking with them on their journey of transformation.

- **Be teachable.** Recognize that some of your thinking and beliefs may be distorted and inaccurate. Be open to hearing from other group members when they see a false belief or an unhealthy behavior that you can't see.

- **Be gentle with yourself, and take time to nurture your soul.** You are a valuable person created by God for a purpose. Treat yourself with the same kindness and love that you give to others. Do something healthy for your soul each day—something that allows you to recharge and reconnect with yourself and God. Avoid putting pressure on yourself to perform perfectly or to have it all together. Remember that your significance comes from who you are, not what you do.

- **Ask for help when you need it.** We were created for relationship, and there are some burdens we were never meant to carry alone. Be honest about burdens that are too heavy for you to carry by yourself, and ask for help. Let others serve you as much as you serve them.

- **Admit your failures, and learn from them.** When we confess our struggles and our sins to others, God's healing power is released in our lives. Allow group members to hold you accountable and support you as you learn to walk with grace and truth.

A Time for Grieving

Welcome to the first tier of lessons and assignments in the L.I.F.E. Guide for Spouses. In this section, you will be focusing on grieving all of the losses associated with your spouses' sexual addiction. It is the necessary beginning of your journey to personal recovery and transformation.

We want you to know that we grieve with you over the many losses you have experienced, and we understand the confusion, pain, and anger you are feeling now. Our hope is that as you work through these lessons and begin to share your heart with other safe people in a L.I.F.E. Group, that you will begin to experience the healing God has for you. There *is* hope for healing, and we're glad that you have decided to take the journey.

In this section, you will be completing seven lessons and homework assignments. Ideally, you will complete one lesson and its assignment per week. Depending on where you are in the grieving process right now, you may be desperate for answers and willing to spend great amounts of time and energy trying to make sense of your situation. If you find that you have completed a lesson before the week is over, we would ask that you wait until after your L.I.F.E. Group meeting before you begin the next week's work. We want you to fully process what is going on in your heart with God and others and not just zoom through this grieving work on a primarily surface level. Take time to feel and to become aware of what is going on in your heart. If you have extra time during the week, read other resources about sexual addiction. Several very good ones are listed on the L.I.F.E. Ministries website.

On the other hand, you may be so overwhelmed with despair right now that you find it very difficult to focus enough to complete the assignments. That's okay. We understand what it feels like to live in survival mode. What we would ask you to do is to spend just fifteen minutes a day working on your homework. Set the kitchen timer, take a long bubble bath while you work through the lesson, go for a walk in the woods, make yourself some tea or coffee, head out to your favorite fishing hole—whatever helps you to relax and think clearly. And then give yourself grace to do what you can and to wait for the next day to work some more.

In my time of grieving there was a passage of Scripture that gave me a great deal of comfort during the darkest days. Thousands of people had flocked to hear Jesus teach and to see Him heal the lame, the sick, the deaf, and the blind. Some of them came because they were hungry for truth. Some came because they were hungry for hope. Others came because they were suffering in some way and they wanted to be healed. And into their lives, Jesus spoke these words:

> ***You're blessed when you are at the end of your rope. With less of you there is more of God and His rule. You're blessed when you feel you've lost what is most dear to you. Only then can you be embraced by the One most dear to you. You're blessed when you're content with just who you are—no more, no less. That's the moment you find yourselves proud owners of everything that can't be bought. You're blessed when you've worked up a good appetite for God. He's food and drink in the best meal you'll ever eat. You're blessed when you care. At the moment of being 'care-full', you find yourselves cared for. You're blessed when you get your inside world—your heart and your mind—put right. Then you can see God in the outside world.*** (Matthew 5:1-8, *The Message)*

Grieving the Losses:

Acknowledging and Mourning the Losses Associated with My Spouse's Sexual Addiction

It was a Thanksgiving I won't forget. I sat in shock as I listened to my brother describe the secret life my wife had been living for some time. At first I was numb. As I tried to sort through what I had heard, part of me wanted to deny what my heart knew was true and part of me was full of rage. She had dishonored me and betrayed me. An overwhelming feeling of inadequacy washed over me, fueling my anger. The scene that followed as I confronted her was ugly and emotionally brutal.

In the days that followed, I didn't know what to do. My world had been turned upside down. Just going through the daily motions of life was difficult. My wife was remorseful and promised to change, but I struggled to trust her. For a while it seemed like she was doing better. I made a great effort to try to connect with her emotionally and to share some of the responsibilities in the home she had carried alone for many years. And I desperately wanted to believe she was changing. What I didn't know was that she was still actively involved in her sexual addiction during that time.

Five years after I learned about her first affair, I got a call from one of the men she was involved with at the time. We separated, and she checked herself into an inpatient clinic for sexual addiction. In treatment she disclosed that she had been in affairs with over fifty different men. We went to counseling, but my wife would never stick with it. As I grew through the relationships I was forming in group, I began to see that my wife was still living in verbal reality—promising to change but never following through on her words. Eventually I discovered she was involved in another affair, and I realized that the marriage could not continue. Letting go of all of the time and energy I had invested in her and our relationship for seven difficult years was very hard. It was a very dark time in my life.—Norm

---

"Melissa, we need you to come with us." I watched as Troy was led to another room with three of our missionary colleagues. The women and I walked into the living room and sat down. I shifted on the sofa, trying to get my very pregnant body comfortable. Inside my heart was beyond anxious.

"We have a very difficult thing to talk about today," my friend and colleague said. "Some very serious accusations have been made against Troy by two women in Lodwar, and it is very possible that Troy will be on an airplane tonight for the States."

I sat in shock. I knew that something was grievously wrong in our marriage, and I had even considered that Troy might be involved with someone, but two women? Besides, my husband was a missionary. Surely what these women were saying could not be true.

But it was.

And so Troy left that night for a residential counseling center in California while I remained in Kenya with our two-year old daughter and a son that was due to be born in a week. I remember sitting in the living room that night after Troy had gone feeling totally numb. I was shocked but not shocked, full of despair and also greatly relieved. I had been praying for our marriage for several years, praying that Troy would love me, that somehow I could learn to please him so he wouldn't be so angry all of the time. I had tried everything and reached the point of hopelessness. But that night as my heart tried to process the grim reality of what was happening, I heard the still small voice of God. "Melissa, I'm answering your prayers." And then His presence enveloped me like a warm blanket.

Over the next few weeks and months I had much to grieve. Our son was born and Rachel celebrated her third birthday without Daddy there. I packed up our belongings and said good-bye to our friends and a place that had become home in the six plus years we had lived in Kenya. I mourned the death of many dreams—the dream of a marriage unbroken by infidelity, the dream of a career of missionary service, the dream of raising my children in a different culture, the dream of seeing the first Turkana accept Christ in the area we had worked in for so long to plant the seeds of the Gospel.

And then there were more things to grieve. I learned that the two women were just two of dozens of sexual relationships in which Troy had been involved. I discovered that some of the women were women I had called friends. I grieved their betrayal as well as my husband's. There was more: the grief of telling our friends and family members in the States why we were leaving the mission field, the grief of hurting our fellow team members and leaving them alone to serve in a difficult area, the grief of bringing dishonor to God's name and wounding many supporters who had believed in us. Oh, the losses...—Melissa

I look back at that time in my life and wonder how in the world I survived. Troy's betrayal was worse than a death in many ways. I kept looking at this man I thought I knew and wondering how I could have been so wrong about him and why the God I trusted let me marry him. I was angry, I was sad, I was numb, and I was confused. Some days I felt hopeful and at peace. And then there were the dark days when despair hung over my head like a black cloud. Of course, there were also the angry days when just seeing Troy triggered overwhelming feelings of rage. I felt so out of control. One minute I would be fine, and the next minute tears would be running down my face. I wasn't going crazy, though. I was simply grieving.

Can you relate to my feelings? __√__ Yes _____ No

Make a list below of all of the feelings you have felt as you have grieved the losses associated with your spouses' sexual addiction.

Did you have enough space? Depending on where you are in your grieving process, you may have written just one word in large print across the page—NUMB—or you may have filled up the space with dozens of feelings ranging from peaceful to murderous.

In the weeks to come you will be working through the seven principles of L.I.F.E.—principles that will lead you on a journey of inner transformation. But before you can begin to allow the Holy Spirit to transform your heart, you must first allow your heart to grieve. The pain and anger you are experiencing are just as real as your spouse's sinful choices. So, our initial time together will be focused on walking with you through your grief. Our goal is to eventually arrive at a place together where you feel ready to join God in the transforming work He wants to do in your heart and life.

Let's start by talking about the grieving process. ***When you think about grieving, what comes to mind?***

For many people grieving is associated with the physical death of someone they love. But we can grieve other losses as well. Dr. Glen W. Davidson describes four stages of grief that we can identify with as spouses who have experienced betrayal in our marriage relationship.[1]

- Shock/Numbness
- Searching/Yearning
- Disorientation
- Reorganization

Let's take a look at each of these stages of grief and the primary emotions we feel in each of them.

Shock/Numbness

I call this the "zombie" stage of grief. You feel totally numb—disconnected from your emotions. The world seems to be moving in slow motion and you seem frozen in a moment of time. There is a sense that the situation is unreal, and your emotions can't respond to the horrible reality of what you've learned. You may be able to carry on with other activities of life, simply surviving, but your heart is not engaged.

Searching/Yearning

In this stage of grieving, you are no longer numb; you are overwhelmed by anger, and you also struggle with feelings of guilt and regret. Your mind understands the reality of what has happened, but your heart can't accept it. You long for things to be "normal" again. I call this the "Why?" stage of grief. It's the time when we typically verbally assault our spouses with a barrage of questions and unload our own commentary on them and their behavior.

The "Why" questions are about them—"Why did you lie to me? Why did you betray me? Why did you do this?" And they are also about us—"Why did my spouse choose this person over me? Why am I not enough? Why couldn't I see what was happening before it was too late?" We search for answers to make sense of our pain, hoping in the process to find some way to lessen the intensity of our hurt. It is in this stage that we most often assign blame. Someone has to be responsible for this loss in our lives. We may blame ourselves, our spouse, an affair partner, our society, Satan, God, or any combination of these. Our overwhelming feeling is anger, and sometimes our anger is so great that we lash out both verbally and physically at our spouses.

Disorientation

The next stage of grieving is the longest and, in many ways, the most difficult. Everything you have known has been shaken, and you struggle to make sense out of life again. In this stage of grief the primary emotions you feel are anxiety and extreme sorrow. You feel lonely and sad much of the time, and the questions in your heart continue. But now the questions are about the future—"What am I going to do?" and "What will my life be like from now on?"

At this point in the grieving process it really doesn't matter why your spouse made hurtful choices. You have come to a place of understanding the reality of the situation, and having accepted reality, are trying to somehow deal with it. It is not uncommon during this time of disorientation for a grieving spouse to move from despair into depression. If you find yourself sleeping during the day, isolating yourself from others, unable to care for yourself or other family members, experiencing overwhelming anxiety, or having thoughts of suicide, it is time to see a physician. You may need medical help in order to make it through this stage of grief without getting stuck in depression.

Reorganization

When life begins to make sense again and a feeling of wellness and hopefulness returns to your heart, you have reached the final stage of the grieving process. At this point in the journey you can smile again and really mean it. Your heart feels lighter, and you are able to enjoy life again. With increasing frequency you feel peaceful rather than anxious, and there is a bounce in your step that hasn't been there for a while.

There may be some days when you experience sadness or even twinges of anger, but they occur less and less frequently. Many of the negative feelings have lost their power to overwhelm you. You are aware of the pain in the past, and your wounds are still tender, but you are functioning again and able to look toward the future with some anticipation of what God has for you.

As you think about these four stages of grief, where do you see yourself now? ________________

I do want to comment that the grieving process is not a linear process. You don't start out numb, move to searching/yearning, then find yourself disoriented, and finally reach the reorganization stage. Grieving is a circular process that involves moving in and out of the different stages of grief over a period of time. What that means practically is that one day you can be numb, the next day be very sad, the following day be so angry you can't see straight, and then three hours later feel almost peaceful. Don't worry. You are not going crazy; you are simply grieving. Eventually, as all of the hurt and anger are processed by your heart, you will find yourself coming to terms with the losses and able to move on with life.

How long do you think the grieving process lasts? ________________________________

Well, my friend, I don't want to dishearten you, but there is no set time limit for grieving. For some people the intense feelings of anger and despair last for a few weeks. Others experience deep grief for months. Every individual deals with internal pain differently, and if you have unhealed wounds from your past in addition to the betrayal of your spouse, it will probably take you longer to grieve.

The good news is that you won't be grieving forever. This is only a season in your life, not the end of life. And although you may not be able to accept this truth right now on your journey, you are not alone. There is a Savior who has walked the road of betrayal and has endured your pain already. It is by His stripes that you will be healed. So, take heart, there is hope.

That brings us to your first two assignments. One of them is an assignment you will do every day for the duration of our grieving time together, and the other assignment is a focused time of journaling specifically about grieving.

Daily Check-In Exercise

Each day as you work through these grieving lessons, you will take a personal inventory of what you are feeling and record your thoughts in your journal using the following format.

Today I feel… *(feeling word)*

When I feel this way the thoughts that go through my head are...

When I feel this way and think these thoughts, what I want to do is…

My choice today is…

My prayer today is…

Let me make one other comment here before I give you the second exercise. During the time that you are grieving it may be very difficult for you to focus your thoughts in a time of daily devotion or meditation. Journaling can be very beneficial to you when your mind is thinking a million things at once because writing helps focus your thoughts. So, I want to encourage you to spend a minimum of fifteen minutes a day in a quiet place journaling your daily check-in exercise and connecting with God in some way—praying, listening to music that draws you to Him, enjoying His creation, reading your Bible or a devotional book. Remember, God wants to love you and heal you through His presence—not judge your performance as His child. He longs for relationship with you, so allow Him to comfort you as you grieve.

Journaling Exercise: Grieving the Losses

On the top of a new page in your journal write the heading "My Losses."

Make a list of all of the things you have lost as a result of your spouses' sexual addiction and sexual behaviors in the following areas of your life:

Personal Losses –What have I lost personally as a result of my spouses' addiction?

Losses in the Marriage—How has my marriage been damaged?

Family Losses—How has my family, our children, suffered because of this?

Financial Losses—What have we lost financially because of these behaviors?

Losses in Relationships with Friends/Family Members—How have my relationships with others been hurt/negatively impacted because of my spouse's struggle with addiction?

When you have finished journaling, invite the Lord to look at all of the losses in your life. Ask Him to give you His strength and comfort and to reassure you of His love. Then call a safe friend or a person from your small group. Share your list of losses as well as your feelings about them with your friend.

I'm grateful for your courage. Thanks for doing this difficult work today.

Next Assignment: Grieving Safely, Part 1, page 26

Grieving Safely:
Asking Safe People to Grieve with Me

My heart was thumping as I walked into the room. As I looked around at the faces of the women there, I was suddenly overwhelmed with an emotion I could not identify. Tears sprang to my eyes. Brushing them away quickly, I hurried to find a seat, my eyes on the floor. For some reason it was too painful to look at anyone. I felt embarrassed and somewhat ashamed to be there. At the same time, though, I felt a tremendous sense of belonging. I knew that every person in the room knew what I was feeling and experiencing. I was not alone.—Melissa

As I write that last sentence my heart is taken back to that first spouses' group meeting I attended five years ago. I remember my counselor recommending that I become a part of the spouses' group at New Creation Ministries where we were living in Fresno, California, at the time. At first I was resistant. Going to a group and telling my story would make the horrible reality even more real, and besides, I didn't want to cry in front of everybody. "Just try it, Melissa," my counselor said. "I think you will find the group very healing for you."

And she was right. The first group meeting was very scary and painful for me, but I experienced something in group that I had never experienced before—the power of relationships. I've been hooked ever since.

Today we are going to talk about grieving safely. Grieving safely involves two commitments on our part: being vulnerable in safe relationships and maintaining appropriate boundaries with others. Let's talk about relationships for a moment—particularly safe relationships.

God created us for relationship. He created us for relationship with Him and for relationship with other people. In the Garden of Eden, God and Adam and Eve were in perfect relationship with each other and with God—naked and not ashamed. It was only when Adam and Eve chose their own satisfaction and ambition over relationship with God that things went very wrong. So you see, from the beginning, God has always had relationship as His number one priority.

If that is true, then we must need relationships in order to experience life the way God intended it. There's just one problem. As broken humans we are constantly choosing our desires over relationship with God and others. Instead of running to God with our hurts and our internal pain, we medicate with all kinds of behaviors. Our spouses have chosen sex (and probably other things) to escape pain and gratify desires. We may choose less obvious relationship-replacements like shopping or eating or working. However, the truth is that all of humanity struggles to walk in intimate relationship with God and others.

So, the first step on our journey through the valley of grief and beyond is to learn how to relate intimately in safe relationships. ***What do you think I mean by a safe relationship?***

On my own journey my experience has taught me that **safe people**:

- Accept and love me unconditionally.
- Are comfortable with my feelings. They don't try to lighten the mood or distract me or do something to stop my tears. They offer a shoulder, and they cry with me.
- Don't gossip about me or my spouse.
- Don't judge me or my spouse.
- Don't try to fix the problem or offer solutions. They simply listen, encourage me, and pray.
- Don't need my love or approval to be okay. They handle my angry outbursts and stormy emotions with appropriate and loving boundaries.
- Are aware of their own brokenness. Humility and integrity are the hallmarks of their character.
- Are more concerned about relating to me and loving me than about giving me advice.
- Are sensitive to the Holy Spirit's work in my life. Only believers can be truly safe people.

Let's contrast a safe person with an unsafe person. These are the people that you need to guard yourself from, especially during these initial weeks and months of healing. **Unsafe people:**

- Condemn me or blame me for my spouse's problem.
- Deny or minimize the sin of my spouse.
- Try to "fix" me or "fix" my spouse by suggesting things I should or should not do.
- Give unwanted advice.
- Cannot keep confidences.
- Only stay in relationship with me when I am happy and hopeful. They are too uncomfortable with or embarrassed by grief and anger to allow me to feel negative emotions and to mourn.
- Are arrogant and self-righteous, unwilling to own their weaknesses and struggles.
- See me as a "project" instead of a person.
- Are unable to see the Holy Spirit at work in me. This would apply both to nonbelievers and immature believers who walk more in the flesh than in the Spirit.

One of the reasons that I am so passionate about small groups is that they enable us to practice being vulnerable in a safe environment. They also teach us how to become safe people in our relationships with others. Before I became involved in a spouses' group, I was very relationally deficit. The only intimate relationship I really had in my life was with my husband, and that obviously wasn't as intimate as I believed it to be. I also believed that spiritually mature people didn't need relationships—that God plus them were enough. We'll talk more about false beliefs and how they impact our lives later, but suffice it to say that I was very wrong. In fact, it is the strong and mature believers who have growing, intimate relationships with both God and people. They live in spiritual and emotional community because they have understood God's priority—relationship. It's a stark contrast to the self-sufficient way I lived most of my life.

And one more thought. As you look for safe people with whom you can be emotionally authentic, keep in mind that right now, family members are probably not going to be safe for you. Your spouse's family may minimize his/her behavior, excuse it, or blame you for it. Obviously, these actions and attitudes fall far short of the characteristics of a safe relationship. However, those who are closest to you may also be unsafe. Your family will most probably want to rescue you from the pain of it all—encourage you to run away from the marriage and the problem of your spouse's behavior. But, as we have already discussed, grieving is necessary for healing. If your family members, in their desire to help you, prevent you from feeling the pain of your losses, your heart will not heal as it should, nor will it grow. And if you fail to heal and grow, you will eventually find yourself in another painful relationship wondering what went wrong again.

So, before you lean on family members too much for emotional support during this difficult time, remember to take an honest look at the qualities of safe people and safe relationships. It might be that right now you need to invest yourself in emotionally intimate relationships with other people who are not so emotionally tied to you—people in your small group, a trusted counselor, a spiritually mature believer who can listen and pray without giving advice.

Let's take a look at our homework for the day.

Daily Check-In Exercise

Take a personal inventory of what you are feeling today and record your thoughts in your journal using the following format.

Today I feel… *(feeling word)*

When I feel this way the thoughts that go through my head are...

When I feel this way and think these thoughts, what I want to do is…

My choice today is…

My prayer today is…

Journaling Exercise: Grieving Safely: Part 1

Take a moment and review the characteristics of safe and unsafe people we discussed today. Now, think about your current relationships. Who in your life qualifies as a safe person according to those characteristics? Who is unsafe for you to invest in emotionally right now? List their names here.

Safe People in My Life	Unsafe People in My Life

(Continued on Next Page…)

When you have finished making your lists, answer these questions in your journal:

- What surprises you most about your lists?
- Does "safe" or "unsafe" describe the majority of people in your life?
- How do you feel as you look at your lists? Why?
- How alone have you been as you have dealt with your spouse's sexual addiction?

Now spend some time in prayer asking the Father to give you discernment as you relate to others, and ask Him to place safe people in your life with whom you can grieve and grow.

Next Assignment: Grieving Safely, Part 2, page 30

Grieving Safely:
Agreeing to Protect Myself and Others by Maintaining Safe Boundaries

One of the most helpful things Mark and I did during our early recovery was to create a contract for safe emotional conversations. In the contract we agreed on how, when, and where we would engage in conversations we knew would be difficult emotionally. We both realized that it wasn't safe to have intimate conversations when the children were around, and we knew that neither one of us could communicate very well after 10 p.m. We also discovered—through painful experience—that a difficult conversation that lasted more than one hour usually had no resolution or satisfaction. So, we established guidelines about the amount of time we would discuss an issue, where we would talk, and what we could say (or not say!). If we could not carry on our conversation within these guidelines, we agreed to take a "time out" and reschedule for another day.

In addition to boundaries for safe communication, I also set sexual boundaries with Mark during the initial months after disclosure. I needed him to know that while I was grieving there would be times when I did not want to be sexual with him. I discovered that giving myself permission to be sexual with my husband when I was ready to do so, gave me much-needed space to heal and to work on myself.—Deb

In our first lesson on grieving safely we talked about the importance of having safe relationships in which we can be emotionally and spiritually authentic. Today we are going to talk about the second commitment on the journey—maintaining appropriate boundaries with others. ***What does the word "boundaries" mean to you?***

Boundaries *are property lines.*[i] They are limits that tell us where we begin and where we end. They also delineate where another person begins and ends. They help us know what our responsibility is and what it is not. They keep us safe from dangerous relationships, and they keep us from endangering others. As Cloud and Townsend say, "Boundaries help us keep the good in and the bad out."[ii] Boundaries are about our choices, about defining our own yard. We don't get to set boundary lines for others. We can only choose to maintain boundaries for ourselves.

We will devote a great deal of time to our study of boundaries as we work through the seven principles of L.I.F.E. In terms of our grieving work, however, we need to focus first on boundaries which function to protect us and protect others.

Let's start with the most fundamental boundaries of safe relationships.

- It is never appropriate (except in case of self-defense) to either hurt your spouse physically or be hurt physically by your spouse.

- It is never appropriate to abuse another person verbally/emotionally or to allow yourself to receive verbal abuse from others.

Let's talk about physical abuse. ***How do you define it?***

For the purpose of our discussion today, we are defining **physical abuse** as *any physical injury inflicted by someone who is angry or is trying to control another person.* This includes pushing, hitting, slapping, pinching, thumping, punching, burning, cutting, unnecessarily restraining, etc. Of course, there are varying degrees of physical abuse, but I want you to understand the concept here. When we dishonor another person by crossing the boundaries of physical safety, we cannot have a healthy, intimate relationship with that person. The relationship will be constrained by fear rather than by love. And where there is fear, intimacy is not possible.

What about verbal/emotional abuse? ***How do you define it?***

We define **verbal/emotional abuse** as *using words or behaviors to inflict wounds on the soul of another person.* Examples of emotional/verbal abuse would include name calling, profanity directed toward another person, threats of physical injury or abandonment, intentionally embarrassing a person in front of others, hateful or untruthful criticism, etc. Again, there are varying degrees of emotional/verbal abuse, and it is often difficult for a spouse to differentiate between a healthy expression of anger and speech that crosses the line and becomes abusive. Remember that real life is all about relationships. Any words or behaviors that damage our relationships need to be evaluated and changed.

As you think about your own life, have these two fundamental boundaries of physical and emotional safety been honored by you and your spouse?

- ❑ Yes, always
- ❑ Yes, sometimes
- ❑ No, not very consistently
- ❑ No, never

Do you tend to allow others to hurt you emotionally and/or physically as a victim or do you struggle more as the violator of the emotional and/or physical boundaries of others?

- ❑ I am most often the victim of emotional/verbal and/or physical abuse.
- ❑ I often find myself violating the emotional and/or physical boundaries of others.
- ❑ Actually, both are true of me.
- ❑ I usually maintain healthy boundaries—not receiving abuse nor giving it.

These boundaries of physical and emotional safety should be imprinted on your heart as two of the guiding beliefs of your life. They are the starting point for emotional wholeness. If you struggle as either a violator or a victim, your first priority should be to begin living consistently within the relational limits of physical and emotional safety.

But how does one do that? I'm so glad you asked. (Smile.) Let's look at some practical boundaries, and then you'll set some boundaries of your own for homework today.

Let's say that you tend to be victimized by unsafe people. For some reason you lack discernment in choosing friends, and so you keep finding yourself in abusive relationships. (Later on in the journey we'll talk about why you are drawn to abusive relationships, but for now as you are beginning the journey, we simply need to be concerned with teaching you how to guard your heart with appropriate limits and boundaries.)

So, let's say that your spouse struggles with anger and rage and is often verbally abusive to you and has been physically abusive as well in the past. You recognize that if the dynamic is going to change you are going to need to make different choices for yourself, so you think about what you will do the next time your spouse blows a gasket in your direction. Sometimes the most difficult part of this process is seeing your options, so let me give you a few:

If my spouse chooses to be verbally, emotionally, or physically abusive, I will choose to:

- Walk away from the argument
- Leave the room
- Leave the house
- Go to a friend's house
- Call the police (if physical abuse is involved)
- Call a safe person to come get me

Of course, there are hundreds of different options, and you will need to think through and talk through your choices with safe people who can help you see your situation and the best decision for you to make in your circumstances.

On the other hand, let's say you struggle with violating the emotional and physical boundaries of others when you are angry or scared. You recognize that you are contributing to an unhealthy pattern of relating that is based on fear and not love, and so you decide to make different choices. Your boundaries might look more like this:

When I feel my anger getting out of control, I will:

- Take a time out from the situation
- Take a walk
- Call a friend
- Do something physically active and productive
- Find a quiet place to journal about my feelings

Remember that boundaries are about your choices. These examples are simply meant to get you thinking about what you will choose to do when your emotional or physical safety is in danger or when your anger is making it unsafe for others.

One last word before we get to the homework. For those of you who are experiencing a lot of anger toward your spouse right now, I want to remind you that anger is a healthy and God-given response to hurt and betrayal. The Bible tells us to "be angry and yet do not sin," (Ephesians 4:26). Your anger is not sinful, but you may be handling your anger sinfully. Raging at your spouse, breaking his favorite golf club or plotting ways to humiliate her in public, won't accomplish anything of eternal value. You may have some temporary sense of release, but it won't last. It's not worth the cost any more than your spouse's gratification of his/her sexual desires has been worth the cost for them. I've counseled many spouses whose uncontrolled rage resulted in huge wounds in the hearts of their children who saw their parent lose control and were terrified. Don't allow yourself to buy into the lie that you have a right to wound and destroy because you have been hurt. We are never entitled to sin because someone has sinned against us. I encourage you, friend. Walk this journey with grace and truth. Express your anger in ways that honor you and impact those you love with life-changing relationship power. And when you fail, be accountable to others, and get back up and try again.

Learning to live consistently within the relational limits of physical and emotional safety takes a commitment to honor and safeguard those around you as well as a growing understanding of who you are. Don't be discouraged if you find yourself struggling to break old patterns of relating to those you love. Emotional and spiritual growth is a process. You take your first step when you begin to notice how you are relating to others and become passionate about walking with truth and grace. Change will take time and require a focused effort on your part, but change *is* possible. I know. I've been where you are. So, be patient with yourself. God lives to show you mercy.

It's time for homework.

Daily Check-In Exercise

Take a personal inventory of what you are feeling today and record your thoughts in your journal using the following format.

Today I feel… *(feeling word)*

When I feel this way the thoughts that go through my head are...

When I feel this way and think these thoughts, what I want to do is…

My choice today is…

My prayer today is…

Journaling Exercise: Grieving Safely: Part 2

On the top of a new page in your journal write the heading "Boundaries for Physical and Emotional Safety."

First, identify at least five behaviors of your spouse that stir up feelings of fear and/or anger in your heart. List them in your journal.

Next, write a boundary for each behavior that protects you and others emotionally and physically using the following format:

- When (name of person) does or says (describe behaviors or words), I feel (use feeling words to describe your feelings.)
- In the past I have chosen to…(describe **your** behaviors and words).
- When this situation occurs again, my new choice is…(describe your safe and healthier choice.)

When you are finished, you should have at least five boundaries that reflect your commitment to the emotional and physical safety of yourself and others. Share these boundaries with your small group this week, and don't be afraid to ask for help.

Next Assignment: Grieving Honestly, page 34

Grieving Honestly:
Acknowledging and Affirming My Feelings

So, what are you feeling today?"

I was sitting in the group room at Link Care with about five other women. All of us inadvertently looked over at the "Feeling Wheel" tacked to the wall, trying to find a word that labeled what was going on in our hearts. The group leader was quiet as we wrestled with communicating our feelings. A heavy silence hung in the air. Finally, one of the women spoke up.

"I'm feeling anxious about feeling."

All of us laughed kind of nervously. We could identify with what she was saying. As I looked at the "Feeling Wheel" I had to admit that I was really only comfortable sharing feelings from the positive side of the wheel—the part that listed all the synonyms for peaceful, powerful, and joyful. Somehow I felt like a failure if I acknowledged that there were darker and perhaps even sinful feelings residing in my heart—feelings like anger and rejection and despair. At least they felt like sinful emotions to me. And I was determined not to be a failure. So, I made a brave effort to turn up the corners of my mouth in a smile and said something spiritual like, "I'm feeling hopeful because I know God is working out everything in my life for my good and His glory." The reactions on the faces of the women there ranged from admiring to disdainful. A big part of me felt heroic in that moment, but deep down I knew something was wrong with what I had just said. It wasn't that I had lied about how I was feeling. I ***was*** *hopeful. It was just that I wasn't completely honest. There were other things I was feeling besides hopeful—and they weren't as nice or spiritual. I left group that day feeling very divided.*—Melissa

Is it difficult for you to acknowledge the painful feelings you are experiencing during this time in your life? Why or why not?

God created us with feelings. He gave us the ability to experience pleasure, anger, fear, and pain. Even before Adam and Eve sinned we know that Adam experienced a negative emotion; he was lonely for a companion. So, the capacity to feel and experience a variety of emotions is given to us by God. And none of these feelings are sinful in themselves. They are simply feelings.

But then things get complicated. We are born into an imperfect family who teaches us both intentionally and unintentionally how to interpret life and what to do with our feelings. Some families are very expressive verbally. Others are very reserved. Some parents encourage honesty. Others model for their children a lifestyle of deception. And along the way we learn what is okay to say and feel and what might get us hurt emotionally and/or physically. Some of us have been in situations so abusive that we decided long ago to shut off our feelings altogether.

So, we find ourselves here in a painful place grieving all of the losses associated with our spouse's sexual addiction and feeling all kinds of things. Some of us are numb—disconnected from our feelings. Others of us can only feel anger in its various forms. Still others won't allow ourselves to feel what we perceive as negative feelings, and a very few of us can honestly share what is going on in our hearts.

Today we are going to work on acknowledging and affirming our feelings. ***What's the big deal about feelings anyway? What do you think?***

First, our God is a God who feels. Just reading through the Gospels will give you a fair understanding of the range of emotions God feels everyday. Since this whole Christian journey is about becoming more like God, it makes sense that we have to feel to be like Him.

Second, it is our ability to feel that allows us to relate to God and others. If we are not feeling, we are not relating. And if we are not relating, we will never experience the Life God has for us. That's what intimacy is all about.

I want to experience Life God's way. Don't you?

A first step toward healing is becoming aware of what we are feeling in the depths of our heart and expressing those feelings to God and to other safe people in our lives. Sometimes that can be a difficult and challenging process, especially for those of us who have been disconnected from our feelings for a long time. So be patient with yourself. I've included a list of feeling words below to help you with your homework for the day.

Daily Check-In Exercise

Take a personal inventory of what you are feeling today and record your thoughts in your journal using the following format.

Today I feel… *(feeling word)*

When I feel this way the thoughts that go through my head are….

When I feel this way and think these thoughts, what I want to do is…

My choice today is…

My prayer today is…

Journaling Exercise: Grieving Honestly

Answer the following questions in your journal using only feeling words. (Do not use the phrases "I feel that…" or "I feel like…".)

- How are you feeling about doing this assignment?
- How are you feeling towards God right now?
- Picture your children in your mind. What are you feeling?
- Describe what you are feeling about your spouse.
- How are you feeling about your marriage?
- What are you anxious or fearful about?
- What is causing your heart pain or sadness right now?
- What are you angry about today?
- What one word best describes your feelings right now—mad, sad, glad, or scared?
- Are there any feelings you feel guilty about feeling? Explain your answer.

Be prepared to discuss with your small group how you felt about this assignment and any difficulty you had with the exercise. Thanks for hanging in there. I feel excited about the transforming work God is beginning in your heart.

Feeling Words

Glad	Sad	Angry	Confused	Scared	Weak
Amused	Apathetic	Aggravated	Anxious	Afraid	Ashamed
Calm	Awful	Annoyed	Awkward	Anxious	Bored
Capable	Bad	Critical	Baffled	Concerned	Defenseless
Cheerful	Blue	Disgusted	Bothered	Fearful	Discouraged
Confident	Crushed	Enraged	Crazy	Frightened	Embarrassed
Content	Depressed	Envious	Dazed	Horrified	Exhausted
Energetic	Despondent	Fed Up	Disorganized	Insecure	Fragile
Excited	Disappointed	Frustrated	Disoriented	Intimidated	Frail
Fantastic	Dissatisfied	Furious	Distracted	Jumpy	Guilty
Grateful	Disturbed	Hateful	Disturbed	Lonely	Helpless
Happy	Down	Impatient	Embarrassed	Nervous	Horrible
Healthy	Gloomy	Irate	Helpless	Panicky	Ill
Hopeful	Glum	Irritated	Numb	Shaky	Impotent
Optimistic	Hopeless	Mad	Paralyzed	Shy	Inadequate
Peaceful	Hurt	Mean	Puzzled	Stunned	Insecure
Proud	Lonely	Murderous	Stuck	Tense	Lifeless
Powerful	Lost	Outraged	Surprised	Terrified	Lost
Relaxed	Low	Rage	Trapped	Threatened	Overwhelmed
Relieved	Miserable	Resentful	Troubled	Timid	Powerless
Satisfied	Painful	Spiteful	Uncertain	Uneasy	Quiet
Secure	Sorry	Sore	Uncomfortable	Unsafe	Useless
Wonderful	Terrible	Upset	Unsure	Worried	Vulnerable

Next Assignment: Grieving When I'm Angry, page 37

Grieving When I'm Angry:
Allowing God to Use My Anger for His Purposes

My anger was very quiet. I really didn't know how to be appropriately angry. Usually, I acted like I wasn't angry and just withdrew from situations, or I let it come out in passive aggressive ways. I would often freeze Mark out of my life, acting like he didn't exist, while I was friendly and caring towards everyone else around me. If you had questioned me during those days, I would have denied how angry I really was. I was more aware of a deep hole I felt in my heart, and I really didn't know what it was about. On the outside I appeared quiet and withdrawn. On the inside, I was resentful, hurting, and lonely.

When Mark's sexual addiction was disclosed, I got angry—but not at him. I blamed the women who had gone after my husband and, in my eyes, seduced him. It wasn't long, however, before my loving group members and therapist confronted me about the way I was avoiding the painful emotion of anger towards Mark. They encouraged me to become aware of the deep hurts in my heart, to see reality clearly, and to express my hurt and anger appropriately. Looking back I see how much my group helped to absorb some of my anger. As I brought in story after story of loss, unfairness, and betrayal, they would listen to me, affirm my feelings, and still accept me. When my anger was shared with group members, I could more quickly access the underlying feelings of sadness and fear. I know that Mark was able to hear my pain more readily when it was presented that way. And I desperately needed to be heard about my pain. I also found that as I talked about my sadness and fear more regularly, it didn't build up to become uncontrollable anger.—Deb

Anger. We all experience it, and we all deal with it in different ways. ***Tell me, how do you normally deal with your anger?***

I (Melissa) grew up believing most anger was sinful, and so I determined that I was not going to let myself feel anger—unless it was the righteous indignation kind aimed at some great injustice. Of course, I did feel anger towards others, but I became quite proficient at denying it, suppressing it, hiding it, and spiritualizing it.

When the Father mercifully unveiled Troy's struggle with sexual addiction, I was forced to look at my beliefs about anger and my own behavior. For the first time in my life I began to understand that anger was not sinful and that it was okay and even best to express it honestly.

Now some of you have never struggled with expressing anger. In fact, while I was intent on being a certified anger repressor, you got your diploma in anger expression. We'll talk later about the two different kinds of enablers (controlling damagers and damage controllers), but both of us are usually guilty of having an unhealthy relationship with anger. God gave us the ability to experience anger for a reason, and in our discussion today we will be talking about how we can allow God to use our anger for His purposes instead of as a self-serving tool for ourselves.

Let's start by looking at some of the most common ways people express anger. [4]

Passive Aggressive	Under-cover anger. Anger is presented in subtle ways—forgetfulness, chronic lateness, "accidents." On the outside you seem pleasant and compliant. On the inside you are resentful. Those who express their anger in this way don't feel safe or permitted to have anger or express it openly.
Sarcasm	Speech designed to cut and wound. The word "sarcasm" is derived from a Greek work that means "to tear the flesh."[5] It is another way to express anger indirectly.
Verbal Abuse	Intentionally wounding another with our words. Name calling, belittling, devaluing, and humiliating are examples of verbal abuse.
Blaming	Blaming anger makes other people the problem and deflects personal responsibility. Blaming anger says, "You make me so angry!"
Guerilla Humor	Attacking someone verbally then smiling and saying something like, "Can't you take a joke?" or "I'm just kidding." Another indirect way of expressing anger.
Retaliatory Anger	Expressing your anger by getting even with someone who has wounded you—i.e. having an affair to show your spouse what it feels like or spending loads of money shopping because your spouse "owes" you.
Blind Rage	Intense anger usually acted out physically—hitting, smashing, destroying, etc.
Isolation	Withdrawing from relationship with the one who hurt you and/or from others altogether.
Depression	Anger turned inward. It is blind rage acted out towards yourself.
Anger as an Excuse	Secretly you want to leave or behave in a particular way, so you find a way to provoke a fight in order to justify your choice.

Using the list I've given you here, tell me which of these ways you normally express your anger.

One more question. ***Do you think any of these expressions of anger can lead to an intimate and connected relationship with others? Why or why not?***

I would say to you that none of these ways of expressing anger help us connect emotionally with other people. On the contrary, they sabotage intimacy because they are dishonest, disconnected, and dysfunctional ways of dealing with our feelings.

So what does it look like to express our anger in ways that build intimacy? I'm so glad you asked! Anger that can be used by God for His purposes is:

Honest	"I am very angry with you right now."
Kind	No name calling, belittling, devaluing allowed.
Direct	Useful anger is face to face, not a cowardly blow from behind.
Responsible	We own our anger. No one can "make" us angry.
Fair	Cruel jokes (in public and private) are off limits.
Contained	We don't get back at others. We trust God to deal with them.
Controlled	We invite the Holy Spirit to take control of our anger.
Interactive	Anger is expressed in relationship where it can be talked through.
Outward	No under-cover anger is healthy. Anger turned inward hurts us or others.
Real	It is dishonest to use our anger to manipulate our spouses.

Now, if you would have told me five years ago that God could use my anger for His purposes, I would have looked at you like you were crazy and probably quoted some Scripture at you like James 1:20—"the anger of man does not achieve the righteousness of God."

Quite frankly, though, **nothing** of man achieves the righteousness of God. It is only when we give Him what we have that He uses it for His good purposes. I'm reminded of the story in the Gospels where a little boy brought his insignificant lunch of five loaves of bread and two fish to Jesus. I imagine the boy thought that at least he could feed the Teacher. But Jesus blessed the little the boy had and fed thousands.

What if we offered what little we have to the Lord? Do you think He could use it? Or do you believe you have nothing to offer Him of any value?

When we use our anger as a tool to try to get what we want—revenge, validation, relief, escape-- we end up feeling a false sense of power and strength that usually results in our wounding other people both physically and emotionally. We also never heal. So, in the end, we are the ones who suffer the most.

I would challenge you to offer your anger to God. All of us judge our anger in some way. We may feel guilty about our anger, entitled to our anger, or something that falls between guilt and entitlement. But regardless of how you *feel* about your anger, the simple truth is that apart from God your anger will not accomplish anything. If, however, you will give what you feel to God, then He can make it useful in your life and in the lives of those around you.

When a man who denies his anger surrenders it to God, the Father uses the gift of anger He has given the man to empower him to place safe boundaries in his life that protect him from harm. When a raging woman gives her anger to God, He uses her anger to help her focus on what she can control and what she must leave to Him. In both cases God's plan is intimacy. He longs to be included in every heart and in every action. He desires true Life for us, and He wants to experience it with us.

So, if all you have right now is anger, give it to the Lord. Let Him teach you how to be angry His way—honestly, directly, responsibly, authentically, and with control and grace.

Daily Check-In Exercise

Take a personal inventory of what you are feeling today and record your thoughts in your journal using the following format.

Today I feel… *(feeling word)*

When I feel this way the thoughts that go through my head are….

When I feel this way and think these thoughts, what I want to do is…

My choice today is…

My prayer today is…

Journaling Exercise: Grieving When I'm Angry

In your journal I want you to write about the most recent time you became really angry—not just irritated, but mad. Use the prompts below to help you write.

The Setting: Describe the location and time of the situation

The Characters: Describe who was involved in the situation. (Also list those who were involved but who were not present at the time.)

The Conflict: What was the primary conflict?

The Plot: Try to identify feelings underneath the anger (i.e. fear, shame, embarrassment) that were fueling the situation. Include them in the account—"I was also feeling…"

The Climax: Describe how you expressed your anger.

The Epilogue: How did you feel when the encounter was over?

The Theme: What did you hope the expression of your anger would accomplish?

After you have finished writing, take some time and evaluate the way you expressed your anger. Were you honest and direct or did you use sarcasm or guerilla humor to vent your anger? Was your anger contained and controlled? Did you protect the other person's physical and emotional safety? Did you stay in relationship during the encounter or did you withdraw? Write "My Evaluation" ***in your journal and jot down your thoughts in answer to these questions.***

Finally, write the words "My Choices" ***in your journal. Think about how you could have expressed your anger differently in ways that were useful to God. Write about what needs to change in the way you express your anger, and talk to the Father about it. Give your anger to Him, and ask Him to make your anger useful for His purposes.***

Be prepared to talk about your anger and this exercise with your small group this week. You've done lots of hard work today. I'm proud of you.

Next Assignment: Grieving Deeply, page 41

Grieving Deeply:
Admitting My Fears

As I look back on the years I spent hoping and praying that my wife would change and our marriage would make it, I know that many of my fears drove my behaviors. There was this gnawing sense of inadequacy I felt as a man because of my wife's struggle. Even though my head knew her addiction was about her stuff, my fear of being inadequate, especially sexually, overwhelmed me at times. It was very painful to think that I wasn't enough for my wife, that I couldn't measure up in bed. And I found myself withdrawing from relationships and immersing myself in work as I wrestled with those feelings.

Another great fear I had from the time I first learned of my wife's addiction and throughout the seven years we tried to work on the marriage was how a divorce would impact our kids and our family and friends. I was afraid that our kids would be very negatively impacted and that our financial situation would change drastically. Every time I thought about the possibility of having to end the marriage, something inside of me groaned in anguish.—Norm

---

"If that's the way you are going to treat me, then I'm out of here!" Troy shouted. The end of his sentence was punctuated by the slam of the front door. My brave front evaporated, and I collapsed on the floor in a pile of uncontrollable sobs.

It had been a familiar pattern for all of our married life. Troy would get angry or offended by something I had or had not done. He would rage, and I would placate and defend. We hadn't had a blow up this big since we had begun working on our recovery, and I didn't know what to do. I was learning that I had no control over Troy's desires or behaviors, and I was gradually laying down my overwhelming obsession with trying to please him. But that day, my feelings were wreaking havoc on what I knew to be true. I felt angry, hurt, and hopeless. But most of all I felt scared.

Not knowing what else to do, I began to pray. "Father help me," I cried. "I'm so angry at Troy right now. I'm so hurt by what he's done and said. And I'm so afraid."

"Why are you afraid?" a still small voice prompted.

"I'm afraid because I don't know where Troy went and if he is going to act out sexually again. I can't bear the pain of more betrayal. I'm afraid that his actions will result in the end of our marriage, that our children will grow up without a father, that I will be a single mom who has to work and doesn't get to raise her own children. I'm afraid that Troy really doesn't love me and that I am undesirable and unworthy. I'm afraid that I'll always be in pain, and that my life will never be normal again. And my kids, Lord. How will I explain to Rachel that Daddy can't live with us anymore? How will I raise a son when I am not a man? Oh, God. Please don't let Troy act out again. Please…"—Melissa

Can you identify with our fears? In what ways?

I want to talk about fears in this lesson because in order to grieve at the core of our being we need to be aware of our fears. I know. I know. No one wants to sign up to grieve at the core of his being. But grieve at our core we must. Why? Because healing takes place from the inside out. If we are to heal at the deepest level of our soul, then we must grieve there as well. The best way I have found to get at the core of my soul is to become aware of and talk about my fears.

Think about your fears for a moment. ***How much do they impact your life?***

I would say to you that we are driven by our fears more often than we are aware of on this journey. Let's talk about some common fears that spouses may experience.

Fear of Rejection

This fear resides to some degree in the heart of every person. There is within us a desire, a craving, to be loved and accepted. But some of us fear being rejected so much that we sacrifice ourselves for another person's acceptance. This fear has impacted my life greatly. I allowed my husband to control me, manipulate me, deceive me, and abuse me—all because I did not want to lose his love. By the time we began working on our hearts and our marriage, I was so enmeshed in Troy that I no longer knew what I liked or how I felt. My entire life was wrapped up in him. Fear of rejection, like any other fear, always results in bondage. We become slaves to the love and acceptance of others. We think we are finding life, but what we are actually experiencing is captivity. The situation may feel "normal" to us, but we are not truly free.

Fear of Powerlessness

Another big fear I see in the lives of spouses is the fear of being powerless or being controlled. I could also describe it as a fear of losing control. This fear is usually accompanied by a lot of anger because anger makes us feel powerful and strong. Often when we are living in this fear we become obsessive about something in order to try to regain some sense of power in an otherwise out-of-control life or marriage. Our obsessions look different, but they are all driven by the same fear. For example, some of us maintain immaculate houses, while others of us focus on our physical appearance and fitness. I might shop and spend without restraint while you save and pinch every penny. A big symptom of this fear ruling in our lives is our attempt to manage our spouses' recovery—setting counseling appointments, reading books, playing private detective, etc. All of this preoccupation with maintaining some sense of control is about trying to protect ourselves from more pain. The irony is that the more we try to manage and control others around us, the more disconnected we become from the only One who can heal our hurts and comfort us in our grief.

Fear of Abandonment

Here's a big one! The fear of abandonment is a cousin to the fear of rejection because if we are alone, there will be no one to love us, no one to accept us. We also begin to question our value as a person thinking, "There must be something wrong with me for people to leave me all of the time. I must be defective in some way." When we are afraid of being abandoned by a person we love, we usually respond in one of two ways. First, we may pursue the person doggedly, no matter how the person is behaving, because at the core of our being we believe that anything, even betrayal, is better than being alone. Or we may disconnect from the person totally—abandoning before we are abandoned.

At least it seems less painful that way. Of course, neither choice leads to peace, and we feel even more fear as we contemplate the possibility of always being alone.

Fear of Failure

When we are driven by this fear, we always experience love with strings attached. The strings are attached to our performance, and we believe that we must behave in certain ways to receive love. The fear of failure develops in our lives when imperfect parents and other significant caregivers tie their love and acceptance to our behaviors or accomplishments. Or we may simply perceive that their love is conditional, putting expectations on ourselves that do not truly reflect their hearts. In either case, our life is shaped by the fear of failure and the ultimate rejection that results when we perform less than perfectly. Those who live in this fear may approach life in one of two ways: with great drive and passion or with great passivity. Some of us are driven, Type-A kind of people who stay emotionally and physically exhausted from trying to succeed in everything we do. Others of us are so afraid to fail that we refuse to try. We rationalize that if we don't attempt anything we cannot fail at it. So we let life go by, doing our best to enjoy what little we get to experience of it. Both ways of dealing with the fear of failure prevent us from experiencing intimacy. Driven performers are too busy trying not to fail to connect with God and others in authentic ways. Those who take the passive approach are professional avoiders.

Fear of Inadequacy

Closely related to the fear of failure is the fear of never being able to measure up. Although this fear can be connected to performance, more often it stems from a deep-seated belief that says, "I have no value or significance. I will never be worth anything to anyone." Those of us who live in the fear of inadequacy usually also carry around a lot of shame. It's not just that we feel our performance is bad—we feel *we* are bad. And we usually deal with this shame by getting locked into a "give up-try harder" mentality and way of living. In the "try harder" part of the cycle we do and perform, trying to erase the feelings of inadequacy we feel, trying to prove to ourselves and others that we are significant and valuable. Eventually, though we get tired. When that happens we give up—medicating in various ways the pain caused by our inadequacy and shame. When that gets too painful or significant relationships are threatened by our behavior, we invest ourselves in trying harder again. The most destructive thing about living in this fear is that we never get to rest; we never experience peace.

Fear of Intimacy

Those of us who feel tremendous shame struggle greatly with the fear of being known. We don't like who we are or what we do. We feel worthless, useless, unlovable, and defective. So we hide. We believe that if others really knew us, they wouldn't love us. So we create double lives, presenting to others a façade of a person we think that they will admire, love, and respect. The true self, with all of its feelings and struggles, is fiercely protected from others by a wall of our own making. Sometimes the wall is made up of medicating behaviors like sex or substance abuse. Other times the wall is composed of good-looking behaviors like community service or spirituality. No matter how we hide the real us from others, however, we are still being dishonest. The fear of intimacy must be overcome if we are ever to experience freedom and healing.

There are many other fears that can dominate our thoughts and drive our behaviors. For you, these might include:

Fear of femininity
Fear of men

Fear of women
Fear of judgment/punishment
Fear of death
Fear of being overweight
Fear of spiders, insects, snakes, etc.
Fear of water, heights, closed-in spaces, etc.
Fear of germs, sickness
Fear of the unknown
Fear of hunger, poverty
Fear of loved ones suffering

Our grieving process is very connected to the fears driving our life. If we are afraid of being powerless or losing control, we might get stuck in our anger. When we are afraid of rejection, we may refuse to embrace the truth about our spouse's sexual addiction, preferring to stay in denial rather than face the reality of betrayal. Those of us who are afraid to fail may never make it past trying to find someone to blame (other than ourselves) for the way our life has turned out.

Grieving which results in growth and healing always involves an increasing awareness of our fears and the sharing of those fears with God and other safe people. It is when we admit our fears that they begin to lose their power to control us. And as we grow in intimate relationships with our Lord and others, we begin to recognize the lies fueling the fears and are able to replace them with truth.

We'll talk more about our fears in later lessons. But now, it's time for homework.

Daily Check-In Exercise

Take a personal inventory of what you are feeling today and record your thoughts in your journal using the following format.

Today I feel… *(feeling word)*

When I feel this way the thoughts that go through my head are….

When I feel this way and think these thoughts, what I want to do is…

My choice today is…

My prayer today is…

Journaling Exercise: Admitting My Fears

On the top of a new page in your journal write the heading "My Deepest Fears.***"***

First, list all of the fears you identify with from our study today, and write down any other fears that come to your mind. (Completing the sentences "I am afraid of…" and "I'm afraid that…" may help you as you write.)

Next, highlight or place a star beside the fears you see occupying your thoughts on a daily basis. Think about what you do when you are afraid. Write down the sentence: "When I am afraid I***…" and jot down some of the things you do.*** (Try to notice at least five behaviors that stem from your fears.)

Finally, share your fears with God in a time of prayer and then with people in your small group this week.

Next Assignment: Grieving Well, page 46

Grieving Well:
Accepting the Pain of the Journey

For the first three months after disclosure, I resisted the pain of grieving. I wasn't in denial about the reality of Mark's sexual addiction, but I was afraid to let myself feel the awful feelings I knew would overwhelm me if I thought about all of the losses. It was easy to distract myself from my feelings because of all of the demands of raising three children and operating my business. Deep down I was terrified that if I let myself feel the sadness and the sorrow, I would sink into a hopeless pit of despair—a pit I would never be able to climb out of—and I didn't want to go there.

Fortunately, I was eventually honest about my fears. My therapist helped me to understand the difference between grieving and depression. She asked me to trust her judgment and allow myself to grieve. There were days that my heart was very heavy—days I felt hopeless. But in the end, my therapist was right. The sorrow did ebb away. I wasn't in a pit. The tears did stop. Life wasn't hopeless. Change was possible. I was more at peace with myself and with others having grieved the losses. I know now that without grieving losses, I could not completely open myself up to the possibilities of what God wanted to bring into my life. I needed to first let go.—Deb

In this last lesson on grieving we need to take a look at four ways we can get distracted from healthy grieving or stuck in the grieving process. Remember, we must grieve in order to heal. But grieving is very painful, and most of us don't like pain. It stands to reason, then, that we will be tempted to avoid the pain of grieving instead of allowing the grieving process to work itself out in our lives.

Let me list the four most common ways we may prevent ourselves from grieving well. Then we'll talk about each one. We may:

- Deny or minimize the problem of our spouse's sexual addiction.
- Run away from the relationship.
- Attempt to fix or control our spouse and the relationship.
- Put a time limit on the healing process.

Denial

Denial is a very effective way to distract ourselves from grieving. If we don't admit that there is a problem or if we deny or minimize the seriousness of the problem, then we don't have to grieve. And denial has many faces. You might be denying or minimizing the problem if your immediate response is to forgive your spouse and believe that he/she will never do it again, whatever "it" is. You might also deny the problem by blaming someone else for your spouse's behavior—the internet, the other person, the media, yourself, etc. If you routinely ignore or repress your feelings that something is wrong or make excuses for your spouse's inappropriate behavior, you are probably living in denial as well.

Some of us do not deny the problem of our spouse's sexual addiction, but we minimize the way it is impacting us emotionally. We may spiritualize our grief away, constantly reminding ourselves of God's promises when we start to feel pain. Or we may disconnect from the relationship in our minds and flippantly talk about our spouse's "problem" as if we are not impacted by it. What we may be trying to do is convince ourselves and others that our situation is not as bad as it really is, refusing to admit the pain we are in or acknowledge our true feelings.

Running Away

Many of us avoid grieving by simply running away from the problem. We may terminate the marriage immediately upon discovering our spouses' unfaithfulness, or we may even physically run away—by attempting suicide or leaving the area without any thought of return. Running away from the problem emotionally may look like staying busy all of the time so that we don't have time to feel pain. We can also avoid grieving by engaging in avoidant behaviors like sleeping all day long or medicating our pain with alcohol or other substances. Some of us run away from grief by getting angry and staying angry. Our anger makes us feel powerful and in control—exhilarating feelings compared to the ache of grief. If you stay angry constantly it could be a sign that you are running away from the pain of all your losses.

Attempting to Fix or Control

Many of us fall into this trap as we begin the journey. We discover the truth about our spouses' sexual addiction, and we are devastated. We want the marriage to survive, but the pain is unbearable. Then our "fixer" kicks in—the part of us which seems supportive and helpful but is really driven by fear. We schedule counseling appointments, buy books on sexual addiction (highlighting the sections our spouse needs to read, of course), and do a great job of trying to manage our spouse's recovery. We may also try to change us in an effort to fix our spouse's problem—going on a diet, dressing provocatively, even being sexual when we really don't want to or in ways in which we are uncomfortable. And it feels so good to have a plan. We are no longer dwelling in the pain of it all; instead we are moving forward, and that feels good.

Unfortunately, switching into "fix-it" mode does neither us nor our spouse any good. Our grieving process gets hi-jacked as we become preoccupied with our spouse's choices, and our spouse is prevented from taking ownership of his/her responsibilities. Our need to "fix" and control keeps both us and our spouses stuck on the journey, spinning our wheels but making no real progress.

Putting a Time Limit on the Process

Grieving is painful, and we don't like pain. So sometimes we will set limits in our hearts and mind on the time we are willing to endure the pain of betrayal and to do the hard work of rebuilding the relationship. We say things to our spouse like, "Alright, I'll give you three months to get your act together. If I don't feel any differently about you by then, I'm out of here." Our limits may also be unvoiced—silent vows to ourselves about how long we will let ourselves do the painful work of grieving. The truth is, when we put a time limit on the grieving process, we are trying to manage and control our pain. Unfortunately, we are also preventing the healing God wants to bring in our lives. God does not work on our time schedule. He sees things differently than we do. When we put a time limit on His healing process in our hearts, we are showing our lack of trust in Him.

What about you? Do you see yourself in any of these examples? Explain your answer.

Grieving well involves accepting the pain of the journey—not denying it, nor running away from it, and not trying to fix it. No one who is emotionally and spiritually healthy enjoys pain. Even our Lord prayed intensely that He would not have to endure the cross set before Him. Only God can give us the

grace to say, "It's a journey filled with excruciating pain, but I choose Your will over mine. I choose the journey you have laid out for me, Father, instead of my plans and my agenda."
What does it look like when you are on the healing journey He has set before you?

- You admit to yourself how bad it really is.
- You feel pain and anger and are able to talk about your feelings with safe people.
- You refrain from trusting your spouse too soon.
- You allow yourself to grieve.
- You seek out trustworthy women/men with whom you can share your soul.
- You begin to recognize that the only one you can be responsible for is you.
- You begin to set healthy limits in your marriage and other relationships.
- You give your spouse to God everyday.
- You give yourself to God everyday.
- You are able to see God's faithfulness through the losses and you reach out to Him for strength and comfort.

I'm grateful for the hard work you have done in these lessons on grieving. In the next few weeks as your grief becomes less overwhelming you will be embarking on a deeper journey of transformation through the seven principles of L.I.F.E. I'm excited about the time we will spend together learning and growing. Today, I have one last homework assignment for you before we move forward in our studies.

Daily Check-In Exercise

Take a personal inventory of what you are feeling today and record your thoughts in your journal using the following format.

***Today I feel…** (feeling word)*

When I feel this way the thoughts that go through my head are….

When I feel this way and think these thoughts, what I want to do is…

My choice today is… focus + look to my good feelings

My prayer today is… that I become stronger in realizing + in no control +

~~slightly~~ apathetic, disappointed lonely sad

scared - Jim's health his choices of [illegible] care + work decision

satisfied, capable, hopeful

Journaling Exercise: Grieving Well

On the top of a new page in your journal write the heading *"Ways I Avoid Pain."*

Think about how you cope with emotional upheaval and deal with your grief. Do you eat, shop, exercise, clean the house, sleep all day, become a control freak, drink, take sleeping pills, seek the approval and validation of others? Maybe you rage and break things or quote God's promises to yourself to get some relief from the pain. You might struggle with fantasy and masturbation or regularly escape into movies or novels. There are hundreds of ways we avoid feeling negative emotions. ***Write down the ways you tend to avoid or escape from pain.***

Now read through your list. Underline or highlight your "favorite" ways to escape. Then complete the following sentences in your journal.

- I am most often tempted to avoid grieving when…
- My escaping from the pain of grieving often impacts my relationships with others in negative ways. My children suffer because…My spouse…My co-workers…My friends… My family members…
- Instead of avoiding pain in unhealthy ways, I can choose to grieve well by…
- What I want my small group to hold me accountable for as I grieve is…

Be sure to share your responses with your small group this week.

Next Assignment: Principle One, page53

Introduction to the Seven Principles for L.I.F.E.

Congratulations! You have made it through the Time for Grieving Lessons and are about to embark on a grand adventure of deeper growth and healing. As you begin your work on the Seven Principles for L.I.F.E., keep in mind that transformation is a process. Be gentle with yourself but honest about where you are emotionally and spiritually as you relate to others in your small group. Also remember that you will continue to grieve for a while. Don't be surprised or disappointed with yourself if you still have days of despair or anger. Healing takes time. Be patient with yourself and talk through your painful feelings with safe people.

The Seven Principles for L.I.F.E. are meant to guide you on the journey of recovery. Don't expect them to be a magic cure for your pain or your struggles. However, if you are willing to surrender your old way of thinking and your methods of medicating your internal pain, then you can experience the life God has always intended for you to have—living in freedom everyday.

Because we come from different Christian backgrounds and traditions, we do not endorse any particular church or denomination. We have no opinions concerning race, economic or educational background, politics, philosophy, or differences between people as long as they claim Jesus as their personal Savior.

What we share is a common desire to be totally honest about ourselves, about what we have done, about who we are and what we feel, and about our commitment to walk with grace and truth in our relationships with God, ourselves and others.

If you sincerely and humbly share these desires, we welcome you in this fellowship of men and women who embrace L.I.F.E.—Living in Freedom Everyday.

Seven Principles for L.I.F.E.

1. We admit that we cannot control the desires or choices of our spouses, and we acknowledge that our lives have become unmanageable.

2. We believe in God, accept the grace offered through His Son Jesus Christ, and surrender our lives and our wills to Him on a daily basis.

3. We become aware of our own sins and weaknesses and confess them to a safe group of spiritual people.

4. We seek accountability and growth in our character as children of God.

5. We explore the wounds from our pasts, acknowledge our sinful choices in response to those hurts, and allow God to transform and heal our hearts.

6. In fellowship with other believers, we develop intimate relationships where we celebrate God's transforming work in us and continue to address areas of immaturity and weakness.

7. As we consistently walk in grace and truth, we carry the message of Christ's healing to other spouses and pursue a vision of God's purpose for our lives.

PRINCIPLE ONE

We admit that we cannot control the desires or choices of our spouses, and we acknowledge that our lives have become unmanageable.

I drove out alone to my special place. Looking up at the mountains, I offered up a silent prayer for strength and wisdom, and then I turned on the tape player. I stayed there for seven hours listening to my wife have conversations with four different men. Tears ran down my face, and my stomach was in knots. Seven years. I had done everything I could think of to help my wife overcome her sexual addiction. I had raged; I had spoken gently. I had spent thousands of dollars on therapy and invested countless hours working on my stuff and our relationship. Seven years. And now my suspicions were confirmed. My wife was still acting out.

It was a turning point for me. I think that day I finally realized that nothing I could do or say was going to change my wife. I was a mess—overwhelmed with the stress of trying to balance work and the problems in our relationship, out of shape physically, and struggling with depression. I knew in my heart it was time to let go.—Norm

---

I looked in the mirror with disgust. Stretch marks, jelly belly, things drooping and sagging all over the place—how was I ever going to compete physically with the women my husband desired? Deep down in my heart I knew it was useless to try. And did I really want to? Shouldn't he love me for me, not for my body parts?

I had tried in so many ways to be the wife that Troy needed. I cooked for him, did his laundry and his ironing, laid out his clothes in the morning, packed his suitcase when we traveled, gave myself to him freely in our sexual relationship. And yet, despite all of my work and all of my sacrifice for him, he sought out other women to meet his needs.

My counselor and I had been talking about Troy's sexual behavior. She kept telling me that it wasn't about me, but how could it not be? Wasn't there something I could do to make him want me and only me for the rest of our lives? And if there wasn't, then what would our marriage look like? I had grown up believing that my job was to keep my husband happy and satisfied, and if I did that, he would cherish and love me.

It was in that moment, I think, that I finally began to accept that I was powerless over my husband's desires and choices, that I was not responsible for making him happy, and that I had been depending on Troy to meet my deepest needs. And that awareness and acceptance was my first step towards healing.—Melissa

We are powerless over our spouses' desires and choices.

Let me say that again. We have no control over what our spouses desire or choose to do.

One more time. There is *nothing* we can do to manipulate, force, or persuade our spouses to love us and to be faithful and true.

How do you feel about that?

You may not believe us yet. Debbie and I work with people everyday who are still convinced that they can change their spouses. They believe they can pray them out of the addiction or educate them out of their struggle. Sometimes these men and women think that changing themselves is the answer—becoming more loving, more submissive, more communicative, more sexual or sexy.

We have all lived where you are right now, and it is a very wearisome place. You try, you cajole, you rage, you seek to please, you rant, you stay silent, you sacrifice, you justify, you plead. It's certainly not a very free place, is it? Your whole life's focus is getting your spouse to love you, value you, and in the process, you miss life. We pray that if you are desperately clinging to the false belief that you have some control or power over your spouse, that you will lay it down and embrace the truth. You will never be free to live if you are depending on your spouse to meet your deepest needs.

Of course, you may have already come to the conclusion that you are powerless over your spouse's desires and choices. Now you feel resentful and angry and perhaps sad. All of those years of trying wasted. God has let you down. Life as you know it is over.

Take heart, dear friend. Our faithful Lord is walking with you on a journey in which He will redeem all of the wasted years, prove His faithfulness to you, and help you see Life from His perspective. The best thing about it all is that you will finally be free to allow God to meet your deepest needs. You will no longer be dependent on imperfect and unfaithful people to have those needs met.

I'm up for that. *How about you?*

Let's talk about being dependent for a moment. **Dependence** is a word often heard when addiction is being discussed. *When people are addicted to substances or behaviors we say they are dependent on them.* An alcoholic is both physically and emotionally dependent on alcohol. His body craves the substance while his soul craves the numbness and escape the alcohol provides. Our spouses are addicted to sex in the same way. They have become physiologically dependent on the chemicals released in their brains when they experience sexual climax, and they also depend on sex to meet the deepest emotional needs of their souls.

What are those emotional needs? There are many we could talk about, but when we sift and sort through all of the needs, we find that two core needs are underneath them all:

- A need to be completely loved and accepted.
- A need to be significant and valuable.

Can you identify with those needs?

Every person on the face of the earth has these core emotional needs. They developed in the Garden so long ago, when, for the first time, man and woman doubted God's love and their significance to Him because of their disobedience. Shame entered the world at that moment, and we have been struggling with it ever since.

So, if it's not just our spouses who struggle with trying to get these two core emotional needs met, then how do we try to get love and significance?

We become dependent on something or someone as well.

Am I telling you that we are just like our spouses? That's exactly what I am saying. Oh, it may look different in our lives. Our dependence may be socially acceptable or look spiritual instead of sinful, but it is there. As we work through the seven principles of L.I.F.E. we will have many discussions about the ways we attempt to find love and significance apart from Christ. For this first lesson, however, I want to focus on how we come to depend on our spouses for our emotional needs. You may have heard it described as **codependence** or **co-addiction**. *When we are seeking love and significance from our spouses we are being codependent.*

But not all codependence is expressed outwardly in the same way. Not all of us are passive doormats. So before you put up your hand in protest, hear me out. See if you identify with one of my codependent friends below.

Pleas-Ant

Self-Reli-Ant

Pleas-Ant Codependents are people pleasers. That's why they are so nice to be around. They never rock the boat, rarely express anger, and always seem to intuitively know what others around them need. They are very compassionate, very service-oriented, and not afraid of sacrifice. Employers love them because they put in overtime without complaining and always express a desire to "help out" in any way they can.

Of course, Pleas-Ants have their struggles too. They can't bring themselves to say "no" even when they don't want to do something, so they often struggle with secret resentment. And more often than not, they find themselves in abusive relationships, victimized and taken advantage of by others who use their loyalty against them. They also find it difficult to express what they want or like, especially when they are with other people. It's easier for them to go along with what everyone else wants than to risk offending someone.

Especially troubling for Pleas-Ant Codependents are conflict situations. During conflict, these people-pleasing codependents usually assume the role of damage controllers. They are uncomfortable with anger, and conflict scares them. So, they do whatever they can to make peace, alleviate tension, and placate those who are offended. Their own feelings about the conflict don't matter. The goal is simply to somehow end the conflict so that everything will be okay again. The great fear of Pleas-Ants is that they will be rejected, unloved, unaccepted, undesired, and abandoned. Their motto is "I will do anything for your love." And it is amazing what Pleas-Ant Codependents will do and endure in order to feel loved.

Self-reli-Ant Codependents, on the other hand, are take charge kind of people. They exude confidence and competence. Highly motivated to succeed and accomplish, Self-reli-Ants are usually more goal-oriented than relationship-oriented. They are great decision makers, and they get things done. Very often they are perfectionists, committed to excellence, who value their reputation and protect it with great care.

Of course, if you get in the way of a Self-reli-Ant, you will probably regret it. Self-reli-Ant Codependents struggle with their anger. And they hate feeling powerless, humiliated, or out of control. When their expectations or desires are not met, Self-reli-Ants will attempt to control or manipulate others to change the situation, using their anger and their intelligence as weapons. In conflict, Self-reli-Ant Codependents tend to be damaging controllers—doing whatever it takes to prove they are right and feeling entitled to their angry behaviors.

What Self-reli-Ants fear most is being inadequate, incompetent, disrespected, insignificant, and worthless. To them having no worth or value equals being unloved. They pursue significance and worth by becoming assertive and self-sufficient. Their motto is, "I will prove to you that I'm worth loving." And it is incredible to what lengths Self-reli-Ant Codependents will go to prove their value.

Now it's your turn. ***Which "Ant" do you most identify with? Why?***

The reason these "Ants" are codependent is because they are depending on other people, and most especially their spouses, for what they need the most—love and significance. When they don't get their emotional needs met by their spouses, they respond in different ways—either placating and pleasing or raging and controlling—but they are both engaged in the same pursuit.

I'm reminded of two brothers we read about in Luke 15. You probably know one of them as the Prodigal Son, and he had an older brother. Now both of these boys lived with a father who loved them and valued them. But for some reason, neither one of them believed that. The younger son thought he could get the love he needed somewhere else. So, he cashed in his inheritance and took off for a different land where people "loved" him, at least while he had money. Of course, that didn't last long, and he found himself in a horrible situation wondering what he could do to get his father's love back. He thought about the way his father treated the servants back home with love and compassion, and he formulated a plan: he would beg for forgiveness and ask to be a servant. No price was too high to pay for the love he so desperately wanted.

So, he returned home, and much to his surprise, he discovered that the father had loved him all along. His rebellious heart had not changed anything. And the father had a different agenda for his son than servanthood. He threw a party in his honor and put a ring on his hand. It was a declaration: "I love you, and you will always be my son."

Now, the older brother came in from a hard day's work in the field. This brother was always working, striving to do his best, pursuing excellence. He wasn't going to be like the younger brother—rebellious and unfaithful. No, he would prove to his father what a good son he was, how valuable he was to the family. And when he saw the party, thrown in the honor of an unfaithful son, he became very angry. His father came out to talk to him. "Dad," the son said bitterly, "I've worked all these many years for you faithfully, never once failing your trust, and you've never thrown a party for me." And he refused to join in the celebration.

Both sons missed it. One decided he would do anything to get the father's love. The other tried to prove how valuable he was to the father. Neither one understood the reality of their father's love or their significance to him. And so they pursued love and significance in their own ways.

The reason our lives have become unmanageable is not because our spouses have chosen to look outside the marriage for love and significance. The reason our lives are unmanageable is because both we and our spouses are attempting to meet our deepest emotional needs in our own ways and in our own strength…and we can't.

Are you ready to admit it? Let's do some homework.

Assignment One - Admitting My Powerlessness

On the top of a new page in your journal write the heading "Ways I Have Tried to Control the Desires and Choices of my Spouse." ***Underneath that heading, write in parentheses,*** (How I Try to Get My Spouse to Meet My Needs for Love and Significance.)

Think about your relationship with your spouse. Think back to your courtship, the time you were engaged, and then after you were married. What did you do or say to earn your spouse's love or prove to your spouse how valuable you were?

How have you handled conflict in your relationship? Do you placate to avoid rejection? Do you confidently assert your "rightness" and justify your angry behavior? What is your goal in conflict? To prove that you are right or for there to be peace in the relationship? How do you strive for your goal?

How have you handled the betrayal of your spouse's sexual addiction? How have you believed you could "help" your spouse? What's been your strategy for making sure your spouse works on his/her recovery?

Write down all the ways you try to control your spouse's desires and choices in order to earn his/her love or prove to your spouse that you are valuable.

Now, on a blank piece of paper or poster board, draw a picture of your dependent self. Use symbols to represent the behaviors you listed above. Be sure to communicate in some way through your drawing what you feel your greatest need is and what are your greatest fears.

Be sure to take your drawings with you to share in your small group this week.

Next Assignment: Principle Two, page 63

Assignment Two - Admitting My Dependencies on Others

Today, as we begin our study into the deeper meaning and applications of the seven principles of L.I.F.E., let's review Principle One.

We admit that we cannot control the desires or choices <u>of our spouses</u>, and we acknowledge that our lives have become unmanageable.

Notice that I've underlined the words "<u>of our spouses</u>" in Principal One. As we take a more in-depth look at this principle, we need to understand that it applies to all of our relationships—not just to our relationship with our spouse.

We've talked about our need for intimate relationships with God and other safe people as we've worked through the first tier of lessons on the seven principles. God created relationship for our good, but our enemy loves to take what God means for our good and turn it into something sinful and destructive. One of Satan's favorite traps for us is emotionally dependent relationships. They are especially dangerous to us because they seem to meet our needs for love and significance, and they don't appear to be sinful—at least in the beginning.

What is an emotionally dependent relationship?

An **emotionally dependent relationship** develops *when one person (or both people) in a relationship begins to depend on the other to meet his/her emotional needs for love and significance.*

We've talked at length about what dependent relationships look like with our spouses, so let's take a look at emotionally dependent relationships with other people in our lives. ***Think about the people in your life with whom you have or have had significant relationships (other than your spouse.) Include family members and friends in your list. Write their names here.***

As you read through this lesson, I want you to be thinking about whether your relationships with the people you've listed above are healthy and interdependent or if they are emotionally dependent. My goal is for you to be able to recognize unhealthy and sinful dynamics in all of your relationships and to begin breaking free from unhealthy dependencies in your life.

Typically in emotionally dependent relationships we assume one of two roles: the giver or the receiver. It's important to note here that emotionally dependent relationships are never balanced, even though they may seem mutually fulfilling. One person in the relationship does all (or most) of the giving, and from that he/she derives a great since of value and significance. The receiver in the relationship depends on the giver's love and acceptance and is always seeking affirmation. It's a one-up (the giver), one-down (the receiver) relationship. And since both people feel loved and significant, it is a very difficult relationship from which to break free.

How do you know if you are the **giver** in an emotionally dependent relationship? Here are some things to look for:

- You feel needed in the relationship.
- The other person constantly compliments you and tells you what a great help you are.
- You find yourself spending increasing amounts of time "helping" the other person.
- There always seems to be some crisis only you can help the person with.
- Other relationships begin to suffer because of the time you invest in this one.
- You are beginning to feel emotionally drained as a result of the relationship.

You could also be the **receiver** in an emotionally dependent relationship. Here's what to look for:

- You talk to the other person everyday, and sometimes multiple times a day, just to talk and connect with him/her.
- The person is your best friend, and you don't feel a need or desire to have any other friends.
- You get jealous if the person spends time with other people, especially if you are not invited.
- This person is the only one who can make you feel better or the only one you trust for advice.
- You do most of the receiving in the relationship. You don't feel like you could really help the other person or be a friend to him/her like the person is to you.
- Your feelings get hurt if the person can't talk when you call or if he/she doesn't want to do something with you.
- You invest more time in your relationship with this person than you invest in your relationships with God and others.

I (Melissa) personally tended to be a giver in emotionally dependent relationships with women while I was the receiver in my dependent relationships with men. Most often you will be emotionally dependent as a receiver when you were not nurtured emotionally as a child and adolescent. Your tendency will be to look for that nurture in your current relationships, and that's why you place yourself in a needy, child-like position. On the other hand, if you felt like you were not valuable or significant to one or both of your parents, you may find yourself being drawn into emotionally dependent relationships as a giver. In doing so, you are trying to gain the sense of significance you missed as a child.

If you are currently involved in an emotionally dependent relationship, there is hope. The first step in walking free is to admit that you are struggling with the people in your small group and other safe people in your life. (Notice I said *people*. No one person can ever meet our needs for love and significance, but a group of people can love us and support us as we begin to walk in freedom.)

Then, if you tend to be a giver in relationships, make a deliberate choice to start receiving. Be real about your emotions. Cry when you need to cry. Ask for help. Hold your tongue for a change, and don't give advice. Learn to feel, and learn to be aware of what is going on inside of you. Let other people do things for you, and don't live a lifestyle of self-sufficiency.

If you are usually a receiver in relationships, it's time for you to start giving. Take two steps back in your friendships, and make some decisions without asking anyone but God for advice. Learn to see yourself as God sees you—a valuable creation gifted for a specific ministry He has called you to. Start speaking your mind and expressing your opinions. Take a look around at the needs of others. Find out what you have to offer, and become generous with your life.

And one more thing for both givers and receivers. Look for healthy relationships that can teach you what it means to be interdependent instead of dependent. Healthy relationships with our spouse or other people are:

- Interdependent—both people give and receive in the relationship
- Based on mutual trust and respect
- Freeing—both people feel free to be themselves
- Characterized by adult to adult interaction
- Limited—both people invest appropriate time in the relationship but also pursue relationships with others
- Balanced—love and compassion co-exist with truth and integrity
- Driven by internal qualities not external appearances

Remember, we cannot control the desires or choices of anyone in our lives. And no matter how hard we try, we will not find our deepest needs for love and significance met apart from Christ. Don't allow yourself to stay stuck in emotionally dependent relationships. My friend, you were called to be free.

You guessed it. It's homework time.

Journaling Assignment: Admitting My Dependencies on Others

On the top of a new page in your journal write the heading "Dependent Relationships in my Life."

Look back at the list you wrote during the lesson. Think about your relationships with those people both past and present.

Identify which of these relationships were or are currently emotionally dependent. ***List those relationships in your journal.***

Beside each name, explain how the relationship was or is dependent and the role you have played in the relationship.

Think about ways you can break out of your dependent role and ***write down boundaries for yourself for each dependent relationship in your life.*** *(I.e., I will call Sally only once a week and will limit the time of the call to 20 minutes, or I will tell Frank that I cannot help him on the weekends since I am spending time with my family.)*

Finally, share about your dependent relationships in your small group this week. If you are struggling to set limits, ask for help. And give your small group permission to hold you accountable for the boundaries you set for yourself.

Next Assignment: Principle Two, Assignment Two, page 68

Assignment Three - Looking Back at My Past

Wow! You've come a long way since we started! As we begin our last journey together through the seven principles of L.I.F.E., I want to remind you of Principle One.

We admit that we cannot control the desires or choices of our spouses, and we acknowledge that our lives have become unmanageable.

We've done a lot of work around this principle. We've admitted the ways we've tried to control and change our spouses in order to meet our deepest emotional needs. We've acknowledged dependent relationships with other people in our lives and agreed to set boundaries for ourselves so that we can walk in freedom.

This principle is ultimately about our powerlessness—our inability to control or change anyone but us. Today I want to talk to you about something else we are powerless over—our pasts.

We've made a lot of choices in our lives. Some were good, others were bad, and some don't seem to matter. Sometimes things happened that we had no control over—scary things, painful things. And sometimes our lives were forever changed by the choices of those we loved.

It gets complicated because our pasts are not just a string of events and memories. Our past is a tapestry of memories and feelings and beliefs that has powerfully influenced who we are today. These feelings and beliefs motivate our choices and behaviors. And as we've learned in our studies together, many of our beliefs are distorted, and they lead us to make wrong choices.

So, if we can't change our pasts, if we are powerless over what is behind us, is there any hope?

Thankfully, there is much hope. For, although we cannot *change* our pasts, we can *learn* from them. And that is the focus of your assignment today.

This will be a lengthy assignment, so don't be discouraged if it takes you several days to complete it. ***Your assignment is to create a timeline of your life, following the directions and format I give you below. You will need a minimum of 4 sheets of paper. Each page will focus on a different period of you life:***

- **Birth to Puberty**
- **Puberty to 18 years old**
- **18 years old to marriage**
- **Marriage to present**

(If you have been married more than once, use one sheet of paper for each marriage.)

On your timeline I want you to record significant events or memories in which you felt very positive or pleasurable emotions as well as those which stirred up very negative or painful feelings.

(Continued on Next Page...)

Use the top part of your timeline for pleasing memories (you feel happy, glad, loved, secure, accepted, significant when you remember them), and the bottom part of your timeline for painful ones (you feel mad, bad, sad, shame, guilt, fear, lonely, rejected when you remember them).

Ex. *Got a puppy for Christmas (5 yrs old)*

______/__________________________________

/

My grandfather died (6 yrs old)

If a memory has both pleasurable and painful emotions attached to it, write it above and below the line

Ex. *First gymnastic meet—won the all-around competition (13 years old)*

________/_____________________________

/

First gymnastic meet—started my period (our leotards were white) (13 yrs old)

Try to remember how old you were at the time of the memory and enter it on the timeline as well.

Be sure to include any experiences or memories involving great fear, great physical pain, abuse of any kind, any sexual experience, significant spiritual events, losses, conflicts, abandonment, trauma, or embarrassment.

*You will be using this timeline as we continue to work through the assignments in the third tier of the Seven Principles, so be sure to complete the work before you move on.

After you have completed your timeline, answer the following questions in your journal.

- What was the most challenging thing for you as you constructed your timeline?
- What was the most painful memory/event you recorded?
- Which memory brought you the greatest pleasure?
- Is there anything on your timeline that you have never shared with another person?
- Of which event on your timeline are you most ashamed?
- Were you surprised by anything on your timeline? Explain your answer.
- Which section of the timeline was the most painful for you to work on? Why?

Remember this is a long assignment. So take your time and relax. If something comes to mind after you have finished, you can go back and add it in. I am most concerned that you write down the events and memories that were significant to you for some reason. So, don't worry about getting every detail right.

I really appreciate your hard work. I can't wait to sift and sort through your timeline with you as we continue the journey together.

Next Assignment: Principle Two, Assignment Three, page 73

PRINCIPLE TWO

We believe in God, receive the grace offered through His Son Jesus Christ, and surrender our lives and our wills to Him on a daily basis.

Pain has a way of either drawing us closer to the Lord or pushing us away from Him. I've had a personal relationship with God for a long time, and I have found Him faithful in the darkest times of my life—even when I was angry at Him and confused about the bad things happening to me. It was in one of those times that God spoke to me as clearly as I have ever heard Him. I was grumbling in my soul about the state of my life and the pain I was feeling over my wife's betrayal. Looking across the room I saw a bowl of fruit, and He spoke into my heart:

"Norm, do you see that lemon? It reminds me of your heart right now—sour and bitter. I know your pain and I see your confusion, but if you will trust Me with the lemon of your life, I will change that lemon into lemonade. I will make life sweet again, and your soul will be refreshed. It's your choice. You can stay bitter or you can allow My grace to make you whole."

That encounter with God has helped me stay focused on Him and His will for my life through everything. It has been a daily choice to trust Him with my pain, but I am continually amazed at how he comforts me and provides for me. His grace is making me whole. –Norm

---

I sat frozen in my seat, looking at my husband. Mark's colleagues had just disclosed the sexual behaviors he had been involved in. I was shocked—numb. Mark sat slumped over in his chair, defeated and broken. As I stared at him, something welled up within my heart. It was a tidal wave of compassion for the man who sat in front of me. I remember feeling so amazed at my own heart. Not anger or rage, but compassion. And then I sensed His presence. It was a silent communication, but my heart understood. "Debbie, this is going to be hard, but this is about what has been missing in your marriage. Trust Me."

On this side of that awful day, I look back with so much gratitude. My Lord, my Faithful One, allowed me to experience His love and grace in that moment. He lived it through me. And the experience was pivotal for me as I began the long journey of recovery. Sometimes the only thing I had to cling to was the promise that God was changing us and healing us, that this was all for His good purposes in our lives. But it was enough. And the ways I have come to know Him now and to have been transformed myself have been worth the pain of it all.—Deb

When you read Principle Two, what do you feel?

There was a time in my life that I (Melissa) would have skimmed over Principle Two and thought to myself, "This is an easy one. I do this already." But after Troy's sexual sin was exposed and the world as I knew it came crashing down around me, I re-evaluated every area of my life. And I began to realize that my understanding of Principle Two was very limited. The choices I had been making and the unhealthy patterns of relating to Troy and others were proof that something was wrong in my Christian life.

Perhaps you are at such a place right now, where you are examining every part of your life as a result of your spouse's struggle. I want to encourage you to continue to ask those questions to yourself and to God. Don't blindly accept the things you've believed all of your life. Begin a journey of seeking to know God intimately as the Lover of your soul.

Today we are going to talk about relating with God. We've admitted that we've been trying to control our spouse's desires and choices in order to get our own needs for love and significance met by our spouse. We've begun to see that we can't depend on our spouses to meet those needs. The reality is, however, that we still want to be loved, and we still want to feel valuable and significant. So, what do we do?

We could pretend that those deep needs don't exist in our hearts. Or, we could find someone else other than our spouse to fill those needs. Another option is to throw ourselves into work or ministry or raising our kids so that we don't have time to feel. For that matter, we could drink or shop or eat or taking sleeping pills every night to avoid the pain and hopelessness of it all. Surely, there must be some way to address those deep emotional needs.

I've got good news and bad news. The good news is there is most definitely a way for our needs for love and significance to be met. The way is Jesus and our relationship with the Father through Him. The bad news is that we don't have any control over how the Father meets those needs in our lives.

Yep. It's that powerlessness stuff again. ***I wonder why God purposely keeps the good things of life in a place where only He can reach them. Got any ideas?***

God wants us to be solely and completely dependent on Him for everything we need. It's the one dependent relationship in the world that is not only healthy, it is required for abundant Life.

Unfortunately, like little children, when we don't feel like God is meeting our needs (a.k.a. not giving us what we want), we cross our arms, stick out our lower lips, and say, "Fine! If you won't give it to me, I'll get it myself!" Some of us have spent our entire life trying to be self-sufficient, filling our hearts with all kinds of worthless things while we starve for the one thing that will satisfy. And it's all because we don't think the Father can or will meet our deepest needs.

And we deceive ourselves. We go to church. We have our quiet times. We pray and sing. We think our actions are spiritual and that we are living the life God wants us to live. But at the same time we are depending on other people for Life. Think about it. We want to feel loved, so we date and we marry. We think our spouse will complete us. But we soon realize that marriage isn't meeting our needs. So we fantasize—if only my spouse would do this or be this way or stop this behavior, then I would feel loved and significant, and life would be great. But the "if-onlys" are not real. So we invest our time and energy into other things like church or service or relationships with friends—all in a desperate attempt to get our needs met. And we believe that we are living godly lives. Our sinful dependencies are hidden from us, and it takes a life-shattering moment for God to get our attention.

> "Helloooo child! Have you forgotten that I have what you want and need? Do you still not trust Me, after all I've done to prove My love? Oh, little one, rest from your weary struggle. Walk with Me. Let me meet your needs the way I know is best for you. Stop doing this life on your own. I want you to depend on Me."

At this point in the journey we reply to God, "But how, Lord? I don't know how to depend on You."

A big grin spreads across the Father's face. "Oh, yes you do. You've been practicing being dependent on everybody but me your entire life. Do what you've always done, but make Me the object of your desire."

"Okay…."

"Don't worry, child. I have given you people who can help you take this journey. They will show you how to depend on Me."

And here we are. Have we told you what an honor it is to be a part of God's transforming work in your life? We are grateful you are on the journey. And that brings us back to Principle Two. ***What does it say? Write it here.***

The three key action words in Principle Two are **believe**, **receive**, and **surrender**. Let's talk about those words for a moment.

Believe is an action word. It is more than just thinking something in our minds and agreeing with it philosophically or morally. It is embracing a truth and allowing it to impact our lives. When we believe in God, we trust Him with everything we are and everything we need. We are convinced that what He tells us is true, and we act in ways that prove our trust. Genuine faith always transforms us.

Receive is not a difficult word to understand, but it is very challenging to do sometimes. It's hard for us to wait. And it's hard for us to get something without feeling obligated to give something in return. But that's what grace is all about. There is nothing we can do to earn grace. In fact, if we try, we are in effect saying, "Thanks, but no thanks, God. I can get it for myself." The key to success on the Christian journey is to become a good receiver. That's why being in community with other believers is so important. We learn to receive in our relationship with God by becoming receivers in our relationships with others.

Surrender may be the hardest word of all to live out in our daily walks with God. We are so bent toward self-sufficiency, wanting to do it on our own to prove that we are capable. The great paradox in the Christian life is that to be mature we must become like children—willing to say, "I can't, Lord. Help me." As long as we resist total surrender of our lives, our loved ones, our expectations, our desires, our choices, and our behaviors to the Lord, we will never be free.

Relating with God—sharing how you feel and being real with Him—is the beginning of true intimacy. God has what you need. He loves you completely. Your significance rests in the fact that He created you. He's always had a plan and purpose for your life. And His first purpose was to call you "friend."

The focus of your homework today will be relating to God, but before I give you the assignment, I want to ask you something.

As you think about your life, what hinders you the most in being able to believe, receive, and surrender?

Often because of the ways others have used God or His Word to try to manipulate and control us, we find ourselves resisting God Himself. All of our walls go up and connecting to God becomes impossible.

Perhaps you saw the hypocrisy of your father who preached at you about how you were dressing and acting as a teenager while he was looking at pornography or having an affair. Maybe someone who should have been a safe spiritual leader in your life took advantage of your trust and abused you sexually. It could be that the pastor of the church you attend has told the women of the church that their job as wives is to gratify the sexual desires of their husbands, regardless of the way their husbands are behaving and relating. Perhaps your spouse has used Scripture against you in order to control you and blame you for the problems in the relationship. All of these situations fall under the category of **spiritual abuse**. We'll talk more about this kind of abuse later, but I want you to become aware of the ways you are resisting God and an intimate relationship with Him because of how others have related to you spiritually.

That brings us back to the homework for today. As you do the assignment I want you to approach God as if you and He were the only people in the world—just Him and you. That means He's not being influenced by anyone else. No one is telling Him bad things about you or trying to convince Him that you are to blame for the problems in your marriage. In fact, He has asked for a private time with you. He wants to hear about what is going on inside of you, how you are feeling and what you are thinking. He wants to show you that He genuinely cares about you and that He understands your hurt and your fear.

Are you ready? Don't worry. He is a very compassionate Lord.

Assignment One - Relating to God

Today, I want you to focus on being real with God, relating to Him from the core of your being rather than only from your mind. I would like for you to relate to Him out loud—not silently. So find a time and a place where you can be free to speak your heart without fear of others hearing you.

First, sing to Him. You may sing along with your favorite CD or sing without accompaniment. Sing the songs that He brings to your mind.

Then talk to Him in your normal, everyday language. Don't try to sound spiritual. Just be yourself.

- Tell Him how you are feeling right now, at this very moment.
- Tell Him about any fears or anxieties you have when you come into His presence.
- Talk to Him about what you believe.
- Express your desire to be a good receiver, and ask Him to show you how.
- Surrender everything to Him—your spouse, your children, your job, your ministry, your marriage, your expectations, your will, your life.
- Tell Him how you feel about surrendering.
- Reaffirm your trust for Him. If you are struggling to believe He can take care of all that you have surrendered, be honest about it, and ask Him to help you believe.
- Finally, ask God to tell you what is on His heart for you. Be very still and listen. He may bring a word or a Bible verse to your mind. He may play a song for you in your thoughts. He may simply allow you to feel His presence in some way. Be sure to write down whatever He says to you.

Make an effort for the rest of the day to stay in His presence—talking to Him as you go about your daily business, asking Him for advice, sharing your feelings, thanking Him when He blesses you in some way.

Then, in your small group this week, share about your experience with God and what He showed you.

Next Assignment: Principle Three, page 75

Assignment Two - Accepting Who I Am in Christ

I am so grateful for the hard work you've been doing as we've journeyed together. Today we are going to talk about who you are and who you are becoming. But first, let's review Principle Two.

We believe in God, receive the grace offered through His Son Jesus Christ, and surrender our lives and our wills to Him on a daily basis.

We've talked about the three key words in this principle—believe, receive, and surrender. Three things. They should be easy to do, but often they are the most challenging work of our lives. And many times, wrapped up in the tangled web of what we believe about God and what we think He requires of us are a cancerous mass of false beliefs that prevent us from entrusting our lives fully to Him.

We began believing these things about ourselves as children when we were not old enough or wise enough to interpret events in our life correctly, and the meanings we took away from those experiences distorted our view of God and of ourselves. Let's talk about four core false beliefs, and then we'll look at the truth of who you really are.

False Belief #1: I am a bad, unworthy person.

Life-sucking, paralyzing, destructive shame. If you are living under this false belief, then you probably have trouble relating to God and believing that He really loves and accepts you. You tend to be critical of yourself, and that often spills over into your closest relationships as you find fault with those you love. You also are prone to get stuck in a give-up, try-hard cycle in which you desperately seek to prove your worth and value for a time until your are overcome with weariness and then you let yourself engage in compulsive and sinful behaviors that reflect the way you really see yourself. That may look like a person who is a well-loved and respected worker in the church who goes home and binges on food to ease the ache in her soul. Or maybe a very successful businessman who spends all of his free time finding and buying new toys or gadgets that he really doesn't need or have time to use. Of course, our spouses use sex to find solace and relief from their shame. And a life lived under this belief is a very discouraged and defeated life. Up one day. Down the next. Always telling yourself you'll do better and try harder, and always feeling more shame when you fail.

False Belief #2: If you really knew me, you wouldn't love me.

When you live under this false belief, you hide part of yourself way. You tend to be dishonest about your feelings and often about your behaviors. External appearances really matter to you. So much so, that you will go to great lengths to look okay on the outside even though on the inside you may be an emotional and spiritual wreck. You also can't be truly intimate with others because part of the real you is hiding out and does not want to be exposed. And you are so afraid of people seeing who you really are that you are unable to love from a pure heart. You always feel like there are strings attached in relationships, that you must behave in a certain way to be accepted. Of course, there is a huge wall between you and God because you don't believe He could really love you based on what He knows about you.

False Belief #3: I can't trust others to meet my needs. I'll have to meet them myself.

This belief feeds the control monster who lives inside of all of us. If you are living out this belief, you are a very self-sufficient person who rarely needs anyone. You don't trust other people, and you resist making yourself vulnerable in intimate relationships. You also find it very difficult to trust God with your life and to rest in Him. In fact, you don't rest very often. You're too busy working, serving, and helping other people with their problems. After all, God needs your help to get things done in this world. Or you may even believe that God doesn't involve Himself in the petty things of this life. It's all up to you to take care of yourself and those you love. Because of this belief, you feel a lot of fear. Secretly, you are aware of your inadequacies, and your body bears the brunt of that anxiety—headaches, stomach problems, fatigue, depression. It's a very lonely place to be.

False Belief #4: Being loved, accepted, and respected by my spouse is my greatest need.

The first three false beliefs culminate in one great lie. I can feel good about myself and worthy to be alive, I can feel fully accepted even when I'm known, and I can depend on one person to meet my needs—if my spouse will love and accept me. And you begin to live as though all of your needs can be met by an imperfect man or woman. You may give yourself away to your spouse, totally denying your personal opinions, preferences, and desires. You may control or manipulate your spouse, expecting perfection from yourself and your mate. Pleasing your spouse may become your number one priority or it may be that managing the appearance of your marriage drives your life. You love with strings attached. As long as your spouse accepts you or does what you want him to, you love him. But the moment she rejects you or doesn't respect your desires, you become angry and/or manipulative—trying to get back what you need for life. Of course, if being loved and accepted and respected by your spouse is your greatest need, then God must take second place as you try desperately to get this need met.

Can you see yourself in any of these thoughts and behaviors I have described? Explain your answer.

You need to be aware that your spouse lives under these false beliefs as well—with one change. Belief number four becomes: "Sex is my greatest need."[iii] The same beliefs that drive and fuel your spouse's sexual addiction are the same beliefs that keep you from experiencing a life of purpose, security, and peace. Your life has not become unmanageable because of your spouse's addiction. Your life is unmanageable because of the false beliefs that fuel and drive your thoughts and behaviors.

Well, if these are *false* beliefs about ourselves, what then is the truth? I love this part. Listen to what is really true about you as a child of God.

Truth #1: I am a person of great worth and significance, for I am created in the image of God for His glory.

Shame is replaced by an inescapable reality: God created me, and so I must have worth to Him. I exist for a purpose. I am valuable because God values me—not for what I do, but for who I am. This truth is most eloquently illustrated when a new baby comes into the world. The parents stare adoringly at their new little one. They talk about who he looks like, who he most resembles in the family, and they hold this tiny baby feeling great love and an urgency to protect and nurture this life. The baby doesn't do anything to earn his value. He lays there, sleeps, eats, poops, and sleeps some more—none of his actions are worthy of praise or love. And the child is not loved for what he will become one day or what he will accomplish in the world. He's not loved because he loves in return. No, the baby is simply loved because of who he is. This little one has value because those who participated in his creation value him. Somewhere along the way, we lose this great truth in a pile full of lies. My friend, you are a person of great worth and significance, created in God's image for His glory.

Truth #2: I am completely loved and accepted by God.

Your head has probably believed this for a long time. The problem is that your heart always inserts an exception clause at the end of it. God loves me *except when I sin.* God loves me, *but He doesn't accept me when I fail.* Some of us have never believed with head or heart that we are loved by the Father, but more often we say that we believe we are loved but act in ways that prove we don't. When we fail, we run away from God instead of running to Him—evidence that we don't trust His love for us. We hide ourselves, our deepest feelings and desires, from other believers, and we try to hide from God too. When we really believe that He loves and accepts us regardless of our behavior and our failures, we will no longer be afraid to come to Him and to expose our hearts to others in the body of Christ. Romans 8:31-39 tells us that there is nothing that can separate us from God's love. Embracing this truth will transform your life. No longer will you be performing and trying harder to obey so that God will love and accept you. Instead you will simply be investing in your relationship with Him because you enjoy being with Him as He enjoys being with you.

Truth #3: I can trust God, and I am totally dependent on Him for my needs.

I need to tell you honestly that if you have not yet embraced the fact that you are completely loved and accepted by God, you will have great difficulty believing this truth. It is hard to trust when we feel unloved. And many of us have had proven to us over and over again in our earthly relationships that when we trust, we get hurt. As scary as it is, however, the reality of life with God is that you *are* totally dependent on Him for your needs. Every breath you breathe is an act of His mercy and kindness toward you. He keeps your heart beating. He keeps the sun shining and the rain coming so that things on this earth will grow and produce food to sustain your physical body. He is the only source of love and faithfulness that will never fail. He is the only person who will never lie to you.

As I write that last sentence I'm aware of the fact that many of us on the journey believe God has let us down. We prayed for a faithful spouse. We asked God who to marry and felt sure we had chosen well and in His will. We question where God was when we were abused as children. We wonder how a good God could allow so much heartache and suffering in our lives. In our humanness, we demand answers and feel entitled to know what in the world God thinks He's doing. And in His sovereignty God often says, "No. I require one thing and one thing alone from you, My child. I will always love you and accept who you are. I made you, and you are very valuable to Me. And, to be in relationship with Me, you must believe that I am good and that everything that happens in your life I am using for your good and My purposes." Faith is the ultimate test of our devotion. I have found God to be completely trustworthy. He's even given me some of the answers I've asked for on this journey. Some things make more sense. Other things I have laid down and left with Him to show me if and when He is ready. No one can convince you to believe. That journey you must take yourself. Try Him, and discover Him as the Faithful One.

Truth #4: My greatest need is to know God and be known by Him.

God created us for relationship. In a perfect world we would have grown up being loved and accepted and nurtured by our parents. We would have felt safe and secure, encouraged to share our innermost desires and feelings. And we would have been able to see God more clearly—to know Him as the loving, compassionate, just God that He is. We would have grown up having experienced true emotional intimacy in our homes and easily entered into a spiritually intimate relationship with our Creator. In a perfect world…

Of course, reality was much less perfect. The hunger for intimacy created in us by God has been fed with emotionally dependent relationships, all sorts of compulsions and life-dominating behaviors, and even spiritual looking ministries. Many of us know God as Savior. Most of us struggle with living like He's Lord. All manner of God-replacements fill our lives, and we've missed the most fulfilling relationship in the world—an intimate relationship with God as the Lover of our Soul.

Living out this fourth truth requires a shift in the way we think about our needs and the way we approach life. We must come to the place that God is our passion—not our marriage, not the love and acceptance of our spouse, not our career or our reputation. And we must harness and focus all of the energy we've been spending on meeting our own needs onto our relationship with God. The truth is that our greatest need is knowing God and being known by Him. No other relationship will or can ever satisfy the deepest needs of our hearts. And let me say this quickly, knowing Him is not about quoting Bible verses and denying painful emotions, claiming to trust God in the midst of the storm. Knowing Him and being known by Him is all about fully acknowledging every emotion you feel, every desire—good and bad, every thought, every part of your heart and soul. This truth is not about some syrupy, spiritualized, and puppy-love kind of relationship with God. It is about a gut-wrenching, often painful, and totally real relationship with the One who calls you friend. Our desire is that you will find that kind of relationship with Him on this journey.

Let's stop and take some time for you to sift and sort through the lesson today.

Journal Exercise: Accepting Who I Am in Christ

Today you will be journaling about the beliefs you are currently living in and the things God taught you about yourself through this lesson. ***You can entitle this page, "***<u>Accepting Who I Am in Christ.</u>***"***

Answer the following questions in your journal.

- Which false belief(s) did you most identify with? Why?
- Which truth(s) was easiest for you to embrace? Why?
- As you think about the four truths, do your feelings about them match up with what your head believes? Explain your answer.
- What areas of unresolved shame still exist in your life? Briefly share the event(s) around which your shame revolves.
- Share about any roadblocks that prevent you from fully accepting God's love for you.
- On a scale of 1 to 10, ten being highest, how much do you trust God? What prevents you from trusting Him fully?
- Describe how you are pursuing intimacy with God. Do you feel stuck in this area or do you feel like you are growing in Him? Explain your answer.

Your last assignment is to share with your small group this week which false beliefs are most influencing your life and which truths you are most struggling to embrace.

Thanks for your hard work. You are walking well.

Next Assignment: Principle Three, Assignment Two, page 80

Assignment Three - The Past Meets the Present: Beliefs about God

I'm grateful for the hard work you've done so far and am excited to see God's transforming work in your life. We are back at Principle Two today for a deeper look into our hearts. Let's review the principle.

We believe in God, receive the grace offered through His Son Jesus Christ, and surrender our loves and our wills to Him on a daily basis.

Your third assignment for Principle One was to create a timeline of your life. You will be using that timeline today, so please get it out and have it ready. In this assignment we will be taking an in-depth look at our beliefs about God.

Beliefs are the cornerstone of our lives. Beliefs drive and motivate our feelings and our behaviors. So, if we want to change the way we feel and the way we behave, we must address our core beliefs. Our beliefs about God are particularly significant in the way we do life.

Remember the key words of Principle Two? List them here.

That's right. Believe. Receive. Surrender. They come in that particular order because our ability to receive God's grace and surrender our lives to Him is based on what we believe about God. So, if you are having trouble receiving from Him and surrendering control to Him, we need to take a look at your core beliefs. There may be some false beliefs hanging around your heart, and we want to give the Faithful One an opportunity to transform those false beliefs into His truth.

And don't forget this important truth. We think we believe with our minds—that if we agree with something in our heads, it is what we believe. But the Bible says we believe in our *hearts.* That's why our lives and behaviors get so out of control. What we think we believe is only in our heads. Our hearts believe something entirely different. And our hearts are motivating our behaviors. What we want to do in this exercise is expose the difference between what we think we believe and what we truly believe at our deepest heart level.

Are you ready?

Before you do this assignment, I would like for you to pray, asking God to walk with you and to bring to light what is on His agenda for you today. Ask Him to guard your heart and to help you see clearly. Then thank Him for the work He is doing in you, for the way He is making you more like Himself.

Please lay out your timeline in front of you. Read through your entries, especially focusing on the memories that involved the most pain or pleasure and significant spiritual events in your life. As you read, think about the answers to these questions:

- Where was God in this experience?
- What characteristic of God did I see in this situation?
- How did God speak to me during this time in my life?
- What emotion was I feeling toward God while this was happening?
- What did God think about me when this happened?
- What did I believe about God during this experience?

Be as honest as you can. Try to avoid answering with your head and the knowledge about God you've accumulated over the years. Answer, as best you can, with your heart. If you didn't see or feel God's presence in a given situation, admit that to yourself. If you were angry at God or felt abandoned by Him, acknowledge those thoughts and feelings. If you felt condemned or thought He was punishing you, make note of that. Also, be sure to record any conflicting message you received—times when you thought God was leading you to do something and your obedience resulted in pain or loss.

Write down all of the beliefs you had about God as you tried to make sense of what was going on in your life at the time—even if you find you have conflicting beliefs. Just write them all down. (And try not to convince yourself that you really don't believe what you've written).

After you have finished reading through your timeline and have your list of beliefs in front of you, read through your list, then answer the following questions in your journal.

- How do I live out these beliefs today? (Give specific examples.)
- How do these beliefs about God impact my relationship with Him today?
- Which of these heart beliefs are true about God? How do I know?
- Which of these heart beliefs about God are false? Why?

Finally, draw a picture that represents your beliefs about God. Be sure to bring your drawing to share in small group this week.

Next Assignment: Principle Three, Assignment Three, page 86

PRINCIPLE THREE

We become aware of our own sins and weaknesses and confess them to a safe group of spiritual people.

One of the first struggles I became aware of as I worked on my recovery was how much I used work to cope with the pain of my life. I learned a very strong work ethic growing up, and a lot of how I saw myself was tied to the quality and amount of work I did. It wasn't long before my counselor and people in my group began noticing how much time I spent working and began to question my motives for doing so. It was a wake-up call for me to realize how dependent I was on my work to help me cope with the pain in my life and to give me some sense of significance and value. –Norm

---

It was my third group meeting and I had finally gotten up the courage to tell everyone why I was there. I shared my story, trying hard not to cry, and ended on a positive note with a smile. "But God is so faithful. He's been my joy and my strength through all of this."

The group was silent for a moment, and then the counselor leading the group spoke up. "Melissa, I'm not sure if anyone else is being impacted this way right now, but I am very disturbed about something."

Embarrassed and a little defensive, I asked the counselor to explain.

"You just shared the very painful story of how Troy's sin has impacted your life, and the whole time you were talking, you had a smile on your face. Even when you were crying, you were smiling. It doesn't seem like an appropriate time to be smiling. Why are you?

Defensively I answered, "I think it's important for others to know that there is hope. God is carrying me through this time, and I want you to be able to see that."

The counselor replied, "I agree that God is carrying you, Melissa, but don't you think being dishonest about how this situation has impacted you emotionally is displeasing to God?

"I don't think I was being dishonest. What I shared was truthful."

"What you shared was truthful, but how you presented it was dishonest. It is a time to weep and mourn, Melissa. Your countenance should be reflecting what is happening inside of you. Think about why you need everyone to think that you are doing okay." –Melissa

Ouch!!! It was the first time anyone had confronted me about the emotional dishonesty in my life, and it hurt. I remember feeling so shocked at the glimpse I had of my deceitful heart. I could identify with how David must have felt when Nathan said, "You are the man" (2 Samuel 12:1-7). Over the next few weeks as I explored why I felt so uncomfortable showing others my pain, I discovered a lot of things about my heart. I realized that my whole family was uncomfortable expressing negative emotions, that I had come to believe that it was bad P.R. for God if His children were not always joyful, and that I had assumed the role of God's poster child—always optimistic, always seeing the best in things, always deceiving myself that everything was okay. In the process, I had alienated other people in my life. They either saw me as some spiritual giant to whom they could never measure up or they dismissed me as a phony. By the time I started going to group, I had become very skilled at being self-sufficient. God plus me was enough. And I judged others as weak and immature when they relied on other people. Of course, I was also very lonely, but I would never admit it to myself. Besides, if Troy would just get his act together, then I would have the companionship and love I needed, and life would be great.

Yep. I was a mess.

Fortunately, God knew what I needed to be whole. So He gave me this group of women, and they began to teach me what relationship was all about. When things got too painful and I would retreat back into my spiritualized rose-colored world, my friends would say, "You're doing it again." And in that safe environment, I was finally able to begin to own my imperfections, my weaknesses, and my sins.

And God cheered.

There is a principle He teaches us in His word. It's found in James 5:16. Let me quote it for you here:

Therefore, confess your sins to one another, and pray for one another, so that you may be healed.

It's a different principle than the one God teaches us in 1 John 1:9. There He says,

If we confess our sins, He is faithful and righteous to forgive us our sins and to cleanse us from all unrighteousness.

When we confess our sins to God, He forgives and cleanses us. We need that. But we also need healing for our souls. Sin always wounds us and other people. And for healing, we need relationships. We need an intimate growing relationship with God, and we need intimate growing relationships with others.

I certainly can't explain it fully, but I do know this: God's healing power is released when we relate to others honestly and authentically and when we invite God to join us there.

"It is not good for man to be alone," the Father said. And He really meant it.

So that brings us back to us—spouses of people struggling with life-dominating sexual sin—spouses struggling with our own sin. If we want to experience all that God has for us, then we must learn to be authentic about who we really are in our relationships with others. That means confessing our faults and weaknesses, admitting that we have needs, and asking others to pray for us.

How are you feeling right now? (Check and explain all that apply.)

- ❑ Anxious because ______________________________
- ❑ Afraid because ______________________________
- ❑ Angry because ______________________________
- ❑ Defensive because ______________________________
- ❑ Resistant because ______________________________
- ❑ Offended because ______________________________
- ❑ Relieved because ______________________________
- ❑ Hopeful because ______________________________
- ❑ Excited because ______________________________
- ❑ ____________ because ______________________________

Because our spouses have sinned so grievously against God and against us, we often become focused on their behavior and their failures. It is difficult for us to acknowledge our own sins and weaknesses—even if we are aware they exist. Somehow what our spouses have done seems so much worse than the things we struggle with.

In my own life I was very resistant initially to the idea that my response to the painful realities in my life was sinful. After all, I had done everything I could to be the kind of godly wife the Bible teaches about and Troy needed. I wasn't the one who had slept with prostitutes or belittled my spouse with cruel and abusive words.

I remember talking to one of my counselors about it one day. The conversation went something like this:

Me: I can see that I've had some codependent tendencies in the ways I have reacted to Troy and others in my life, but I really don't see how that is sinful—unhealthy maybe, but not sinful.

Counselor: Tell me, Melissa, as you were trying to please Troy all those years, did you ever lie to protect yourself from his anger?

Me: (Hesitantly) Well...uh...yes, I have to say I did.

Counselor: Is lying sinful?

Me: (Sheepishly) Okay. I see your point.

As I have continued to grow through the years and have given God permission to reveal sin and weakness in my heart, I have discovered a great many things I needed to confess and be accountable for with my small group. We'll be talking more about the sinful ways we respond to pain and betrayal in Principles 4 and 5. For now, however, my prayer for you is that you would begin to become aware of your own sins and weakness and that you would begin sharing your struggles with a safe group of spiritual people.

And one last word before we get to the homework. When we talk about confession, we are speaking about being transparent about our sins and failures. I want you to be transparent about your faults and weaknesses because being transparent is a great first step toward building intimate relationships. However, as you grow, in order for real change to take place in your life, you will need to move from transparency to authenticity. ***What's the difference between the two?***

Transparency is about confessing thoughts and behaviors. "I just want to let you know, guys, that I seriously contemplated murdering my spouse's affair partner today. I made a plan and everything." Or, "I was so mad, I took the credit card and spent $1000.00 on myself today. I thought my spouse owed me after all he's done."

You are being transparent about your sinful thoughts and behaviors; you've confessed them, but you are not yet being authentic. Authenticity is about the heart. It moves beyond confession to a desire for change. Notice the difference.

"I felt so lonely and so resentful today as I thought about my spouse's affair. It has cost us everything, and I'm so tired of the feelings of inadequacy and pain. I have to confess I contemplated murder. I made a plan. I wanted revenge. Fortunately, I came to my senses, but I feel so weak sometimes. I hate not being in control, I hate feeling so powerless and so invaluable. Sometimes God seems so far away. I want to depend on Him for my needs. Would you all pray for me?

Or, "I'm so ashamed of myself. I let my anger control me today. I got so mad I spent a thousand bucks on the credit card on stuff I didn't even need. I hate it when I get so out of control. I feel worse after it's all over than I did before. I should have called one of you, but I didn't want to stop being angry. It felt so good, so empowering, so much better than feeling helpless. I know I'll have to apologize and make amends by taking all of the stuff back. Would you guys hold me accountable?

When we are being transparent, we are only sharing our thoughts and behaviors. We don't change because we haven't admitted what is driving those thoughts and behaviors, and we don't ask for help to change. We may feel accepted and loved, but underneath our transparency may be an unwillingness to change or a victim mentality that tells us change is not possible. That's what happens in the lives of people who come to group and report the same sinful thoughts and behaviors week after week. They are being transparent, but they have not become authentic.

When we are authentic, we acknowledge the feelings and beliefs behind our behaviors. We express our desire to align our hearts with the heart of God, and we ask for help in doing that. Authentic people experience lasting change. Their hearts are connected in intimate relationship with God and others, and they are transformed.

So, become aware of your own sins and weaknesses and confess them to members of your small group. Start with transparency as you build relationships, but don't stay there. Take the risk and entrust your heart to God and others so that you can grow and heal.

Now, it's time for homework.

Assignment One - Relating to Others Authentically

Today you will be taking a deep look into your own heart and life. *Start by inviting God to join you. Find a quiet place and sit down together.*

Tell the Father you are going to take a look at <u>your</u> heart today instead of focusing on your spouse's sinful behavior. Express how you are feeling about focusing on your sins and weaknesses—anger, defensiveness, shame, outrage, relief—whatever it is you are feeling.

Ask God to help you see His perspective, and ask Him to open your eyes to anything interfering in your relationship with Him.

Then, make a list of anything He brings to mind.

When you have finished, read the list you have written and talk to God about it. Express any sorrow you feel, any shame, any resistance to change. And then give Him permission to change whatever He needs to in you to make you look more like Him.

The hardest part of this assignment comes next. In your small group this week, share about the sins God has made you aware of as you have opened your heart to Him. If you feel safe enough, tell your group about the thoughts and feelings motivating your sinful choices. Also, allow group members to pray for you.

Thanks for being teachable this week. I'm grateful for your honesty.

Next Assignment: Principle Four, page 89

Assignment Two - Relating to My Spouse Authentically

Welcome back to Principle Three. Are you ready to go deeper? Let's review the principle again.

We become aware of our own sins and weaknesses and confess them to a safe group of spiritual people.

You can probably already tell by the title of this assignment where we are headed today. We've practiced being authentic with the people in our small group, and now we need to begin changing the way we relate to our spouses. That means being real in everything we say and do. Not cruel or manipulative, not syrupy or placating—real.

Real people acknowledge what they are feeling appropriately.
Real people don't have hidden agendas. They express their desires verbally.
Real people have personal boundaries that help them walk with grace and truth.
Real people admit when they are wrong and make amends.

You would think that our relationships with our spouses would be the easiest for us to be real in. Usually, it's quite the opposite. There are too many things at stake—feeling loved and significant, for example—for us to risk being authentic. That's why this is your second assignment on Principle Two. By now you've developed loving and authentic relationships in group that will provide a solid place from which to begin relating in real ways with your spouse.

I recognize that your spouse may not have chosen to take the journey with you. Your spouse may be in denial about his/her addiction, and you may even be separated. Whatever the situation, you can still relate to your spouse authentically, albeit with appropriate boundaries.

So, let's talk about what an authentic relationship with your spouse looks like.

1. **When we are authentically relating to our spouses, we acknowledge and express what we are feeling appropriately.**

There are three key words in this sentence—acknowledge, express, appropriately. First of all, we must be aware of what we are feeling in the midst of a situation. Are we angry? What emotion is behind the anger? Maybe fear, maybe hurt. Then, we must express our feelings to our spouse. Feelings kept inside have the power to do us and our relationships great harm. Physically our bodies may bear the brunt of our unexpressed feelings. Migraines, stomach aches, chronic diarrhea, chest palpitations, chest pain—all can be triggered by unresolved and unexpressed feelings. Emotionally, intimacy is blocked when we fail to express our hearts because our spouses don't know what is really going on inside of us.

But don't forget the "appropriately" part. Feelings should always be owned (I.e. "I feel..." instead of "you make me so...") and explained (I feel...about...because...). Appropriate expression of feelings builds intimacy. Inappropriate expression of feelings builds walls.

Tell me, what are some ways you think we might be tempted to express our feelings inappropriately?

Screaming, yelling, throwing things, hitting, punching, biting, destroying things—none of these build intimacy. Withdrawing, giving angry looks, crying hysterically, begging, and placating don't build intimacy either. I'm not saying that there is not a place for expressing your feelings in some of these ways when you are alone, but if you are trying to build an authentic relationship with your spouse, these ways won't get you there.

Remember, intimacy is about knowing and being known. It is much more real to say, "I am so afraid to be alone that I pursue you instead of giving you the space you need to grow," than to nag your spouse about telling you how he/she is doing in recovery. There's a chance for intimacy if you can honestly admit, "The reason I get so angry with you when you watch TV instead of talking to me is that I feel insignificant and worthless and that hurts," rather than continuing to lecture your spouse about needing to spend time with the family.

2. When we are relating authentically to our spouses, we communicate our expectations and desires verbally.

"I wish *somebody* in this family would take the trash out."

Do you know what that is? That's code language. And it's very shaming. If the "somebody" you are talking about is your spouse, then you just demoted him/her. Your spouse is no longer a valuable person, he/she is just a "somebody."

Authentic people express their desires and expectations openly, with no hidden agendas. They don't use coded language. They are direct and honest. "Honey, I'm feeling annoyed because the trashcan is full and you agreed to take the trash out for me this morning. I would appreciate it if you could take care of it now." By being honest and owning your feeling, you've given your spouse a chance to apologize and follow through on the task rather than creating an unsafe environment in which your spouse feels defensive and put down.

You could state this principle in a different way as well: "Say what you mean, and mean what you say." Become a person of integrity. Don't use your speech to try to manipulate or control others. Use your words to build intimacy.

I do want to point out that even when we communicate our expectations and desires verbally, our spouses may choose not to honor our request. We can't control our spouses' choices, but we can do our best to walk authentically on our own journey.

3. When we are relating to our spouses authentically, we have personal boundaries that help us walk with kindness and integrity.

Boundaries. Relational limits. Lines that define where our responsibility begins and ends. We've talked about boundaries as they relate to the physical and emotional safety of others and us. We'll talk more about boundaries when we get to Principle Six, but I do want to mention a few relational boundaries that will greatly enhance your ability to build intimacy with your spouse. Since boundaries are for us, I'll write them in the first person.

- **I will not nag.** Nagging is unexpressed fear. Every time we nag our spouses, we are silently screaming, "You are incompetent," at least, that's what they hear. Nagging is also very parental. Adults don't nag other adults. Adults nag irresponsible and forgetful children. So, if you want to build authentic relationship with your spouse, nagging must be put aside.

Are the "but what abouts" forming in your mind? I know that your spouse may be irresponsible and forgetful. Many of our spouses have some growing up to do emotionally. However, there are many creative ways to approach irresponsibility without nagging. Does your spouse always leave his clothes on the floor? State your desire for him to put his clothes away, and explain to him that you will assume any clothes left on the floor for more than a day are unwanted and will donate them to charity. Does your spouse struggle with overspending? State your concern about the situation and your fear that your financial reputation will be affected by her spending. Then explain to her that the next time she exceeds an agreed-upon budget, your choice will be to relieve her of the credit cards. (These are just a couple of ideas. You will need to be creative in the way you set limits in order to avoid nagging.)

- **I will not rescue.** One of the biggest ways we prevent true intimacy in our relationships with our spouses is by rescuing them from the consequences of their choices. We rescue because we feel important and powerful. We also rescue because if our spouses fail, we won't get our needs met. Rescuing enables our spouses to remain child-like and immature in the way they approach life and relationships. The longer we rescue, the longer we put off experiencing authentic relationship with our spouse.

  Don't shield your spouse from the consequences of his/her behaviors. Don't make excuses for your spouse, and don't act as a buffer between your spouse and other people. Allow your spouse to feel the full impact of his/her choices. Your spouse will probably be angry and resentful when you change your patterns of relating. But hang in there. The only hope for intimacy in your marriage is for you and your spouse to begin relating to each other as adults.

- **I will not gossip.** On the other side of rescuing is gossiping. "Do you know what my spouse did?" Gossip often is unexpressed anger. Instead of expressing our feelings appropriately, we talk about our spouses. We want validation and empathy. We want to feel good about ourselves, so we invest in tearing down our spouses. If we are believers, we may spiritualize it—"Please pray for my spouse because…"—but our motives are not pure.

  Your spouse already feels worthless, condemned, and unlovable. If you want to build intimacy, you need to become a safe person for your spouse to share his/her heart with. And if your spouse knows that what is shared between you will be shared in other places, your spouse will never attempt to relate to you authentically.

  If you have to talk about something with others, talk about yourself. Talk about what you've been feeling and the ways you've been behaving. That's the opposite of gossip. It's called intimacy.

- **I will not lie.** We of all people should know how dishonesty destroys trust and prevents intimacy. And yet, many of us struggle with lying, especially in our relationships with our spouses. We lie for one and only one reason: we are afraid of something. We may fear hurting someone else's feelings. We may be afraid of being wrong or failing. We may fear the anger of our spouse, physical or emotional abuse, the pain of being rejected. We may be terrified that if we are honest, we will be abandoned.

No matter what we are afraid of, however, authentic relationships cannot happen in an environment of dishonesty and deception. If your situation is unsafe, and you cannot be honest without receiving physical or emotional abuse, it is time for you to put a healthy distance between you and your spouse. A time of separation may be the only thing that can help you feel safe enough to begin being honest with yourself and others.

If, however, you struggle with being dishonest because of your own emotional fears, then it is time to take a step toward intimacy by being truthful in everything. Stop pretending you aren't bothered or upset. Stop hiding your own secret behaviors. Stop telling the children everything is okay. Oh, my friend. We will never experience the intimacy we crave apart from truth.

4. When we are relating authentically with our spouses, we admit our failures and make amends.

After I discovered all of the sinful and hurtful sexual behaviors Troy had been doing, I felt strangely empowered. It was a good-bad thing. The knowledge of his betrayal helped me to break free from many of the enabling, dependent patterns of relating I had been engaging in for a long time. But, I also began to feel entitled—entitled to my cruel words aimed at his direction, entitled to spend as much as he had spent on his addiction, entitled to hurt him back because he had hurt me.

But that was not God's way, nor His best plan for me. I've said it before, and I'll say it again. We are not entitled to do anything we want to just because we've been hurt. If we persist in using our spouses' failures as an excuse for our sin, we will never be free, and we will never experience intimacy.

Authentic relationships are honest. They are honest about failures as well as successes. In an authentic relationship, both people seek the good of each other. And they walk, not perfectly, but consistently in grace and truth—kindness and integrity.

What that means for us is that as we approach the awesome task of building an authentic relationship with our spouses, we must own our wrong choices, ask for forgiveness, and make amends where necessary. Yes, it is hard to do in light of the way our spouses have sinned against us. We feel like our sin could not possibly compare to what they've done. ***But let me ask you this: whose sin put Christ on the cross?***

The answer is both of your sins did. I want to see you whole, regardless of the choices your spouse makes in this life. I want to see you enjoy intimate relationships with God and others whether or not your marriage lasts. And you won't be able to have healing and intimacy if you resist taking responsibility for your sinful choices in your marriage relationship. I don't want you to apologize for stuff that's not yours, but I do want you to search your heart, and allow the Father to show you any ways in which you need to accept responsibility for wrongs done and to be willing to make amends.

Before we get to our assignment today, I do need to clarify some things. First, I want to recognize that all of our spouses are at different places in their own journeys. Some have embraced recovery and are passionately pursuing God with all that they are. Others are dabbling at the hard work of transformation, while still others are really not working at all. Some of our spouses are in denial. They don't believe they have a problem. So, when we talk about relating to our spouses authentically, I am talking about what we have power over—our own behavior and choices.

We cannot control or change what our spouses desire or choose to do. But we can walk our own journeys with grace and truth. We can choose to stop lying to protect ourselves or our reputation. We can choose to be angry without being physically or verbally abusive. We can decide not to nag or rescue or gossip. We can choose to deal with our pain in healthy ways instead of overeating or drinking or shopping. And we can choose to admit when we fail—even to a spouse who denies any sinfulness on his part—and to ask for forgiveness.

Are you open to admitting that you fail sometimes?

Are you willing to begin thinking about how and when you need to deal with those failures in your relationship with your spouse?

And one more thought. If you choose to walk with integrity in your marriage—owning your failures and asking for forgiveness when appropriate—don't expect your spouse to reciprocate. Your spouse may very well soften towards you and begin to relate to you more authentically. However, your spouse may also use your honesty against you as a way to justify his/her behavior or blame you for his/her choices. It all depends on where your spouse is on his/her journey.

But don't worry. God will honor your commitment to be authentic regardless of your spouse's choices, and He'll give you wisdom and discernment to know when and how to deal with your failures in your marriage relationship.

That's a good place to stop for today. It's time for homework.

Your first assignment in Principle 3 was to make a list of different sins and struggles that were interfering with an intimate relationship with God. Today we are going to focus on those behaviors that interfere with an intimate relationship with your spouse.

Start by spending some time in prayer. Acknowledge any feelings or fears, resentment, or resistance you are feeling as you do this assignment, and tell God about what is going on in your heart. Deliberately choose to submit your heart to His inspection, and invite Him to show you any of <u>your</u> choices or behaviors that are preventing you and your spouse from experiencing emotional intimacy in your marriage relationship.

Write down any behaviors, attitudes, or words God brings to your thoughts during this time of prayer. Then answer the following questions in your journal:

- When I think about these behaviors and choices, I feel…
- When I think about confessing these behaviors and choices to my spouse, I feel…
- In the past when I have confessed sins and struggles to my spouse he/she has responded by…
- Presently I feel (safe/unsafe) admitting my failures to my spouse because…
- As I think about this list of choices and behaviors interfering with my relationship with my spouse, what I feel I need to do is…

In your small group this week, talk to your friends about the things you do that prevent you and your spouse from relating in an emotionally intimate way. Ask your group for help in discerning whether or not the time is right for you to confess your failures to your spouse.

Also, if you struggled to see any failures on your part or are feeling very defensive as a result of this assignment, talk to your small group about these feelings as well.

Thanks for doing this difficult and stretching assignment. I'm proud of you for wanting to grow up in Him.

Next Assignment: Principle Four, Assignment Two, page 93

Assignment Three - The Past Meets the Present: Exploring My Desires and Fears

My prayer for you as you take another look at your timeline today is that God would give you insight and understanding as we explore your fears and where they came from. I also pray that He will be your comfort and your strength as you look back at painful moments in your life.

Today we will be exploring the roots of our sins and weaknesses. Let's review Principle Three.

We become aware of our own sins and weaknesses and confess them to a safe group of spiritual people.

All of us, as we have learned, interpret our life experiences. Memories have meaning, and the beliefs and feelings and messages we take away from those memories shape our lives. We learn to define some kinds of experiences as "good" and others as "bad." Usually, we define events by the kinds of feelings they stir up within us. Some experiences give us "warm fuzzies." We feel safe, loved, significant, proud, strong, secure, well. Other events in our lives bring up feelings we would rather not feel—lonely, insecure, unsafe, incompetent, unloved, unaccepted, weak, insignificant, bad.

As we grow, we begin to categorize these two kinds of experiences. We want the kind that gives us pleasant feelings, and we try to avoid the kind of events that bring up very painful feelings. In short, as Larry Crabb describes it, we define for ourselves what is Life and Death to us.[iv] We then begin to live for those experiences which seem like Life and try desperately to prevent what seems like death from happening to us again. Without our knowing it, we become slaves to our desires and our fears.

What exactly does that look like? Let's say as the child of an alcoholic father you grow up in constant fear of your father's explosive anger and violent rages. What you long for is security and love, and so you begin to behave in ways that minimize your chances of experiencing your father's anger while at the same time doing whatever you can to earn his love and approval. And you grow up, believing that the way you live is normal and good. What in reality is codependence seems like Life to you, and what you think is the spiritual gift of mercy or a great ability to get along with anyone is really all about trying to avoid the rejection and insecurity that feel like death to you.

But what's so bad about avoiding pain?

Well, there's only one problem with living your life trying to avoid what is death to you. As a believer, you are called to deny yourself, take up your cross, and follow Christ (Luke 9:23). What if denying yourself brings up feelings of worthlessness or insignificance? What if taking up your cross involves feeling weak and inadequate and powerless? What if following God means you are rejected and alone? The dilemma then becomes, "How can I be a disciple of Christ and still avoid what seems like death to me?"

And the answer is…you can't.

So, if your desire is to have an intimate, growing relationship with the Father, you must begin the journey of unhooking your heart from the passions of Life and Death and allow your passion to become God. The difference will be that increasingly the Holy Spirit will guide and direct your life instead of your desires and fears controlling your thoughts and behaviors.

It is a journey—not a one-time event—for you to redefine what is Life to you and to fully believe there is no Death for those of us in Christ Jesus. And it's a journey we'll start today.

Please lay out your timeline in front of you. First, read through the top portion of your timeline—the pleasant and positive memories.

As you read, ask yourself this question: What did I gain as a result of this experience? Words like acceptance, love, safety, significance, value, etc. are examples of feelings you may have felt. ***Write down the heading "Life" in your journal, and jot down the words that come to your mind as you read through the top portion of your timeline.***

Now read through the bottom portion of your timeline where you recorded memories that brought up negative, painful feelings. It is our interpretation of the most painful experiences in our life that most often result in our core false beliefs. ***As you read, ask yourself this question: What did I lose as a result of this experience?***

Examples might be innocence, sense of worth, sense of identity, love, security, trust, etc. ***In your journal write the heading "Death—Loss of:" and list the things you see as losses as you read through the lower half of your timeline.***

When you are finished, answer the following questions in your journal.

- As I look back over my life, I see I have defined Life as…
- The way I have defined death as I have interpreted the painful events of my life is the loss of…
- Because __________ (fill in the blank) is Life to me, in my relationships with others I always seek to…
- Because __________ (fill in the blank) is death to me, in my relationship with my children and my spouse I tend to…
- As I think about what death is to me, my greatest fear is...

Extra Credit Work: (smile)

- Life and Death for my mom were…
- Life and Death for my dad were…
- I defined Life like my _________ (choose mom or dad).
- I defined Death like my _______ (choose mom or dad).

(Continued on Next Page…)

Now let's take this assignment to the present day. ***Think of a current situation that feels like "Death" to you. Make it one that still evokes painful emotions. In your journal write the word "Experience" and briefly summarize the event or situation.***

Next write the word "Interpretation" and talk about how you have interpreted the situation—how you have viewed the thoughts and motives of the other person and what you have told yourself about them, about yourself, and about God.

The next word is "Fears." Write about what fears, doubts, and anxieties the situation is triggering for you. (Include physical, emotional, and spiritual fears.)

Fourth is "Feelings." Now write about all of the things you felt as the experience was unfolding. Re-live the situation and jot down what you felt along the way.

Finally, write the word "Evaluation." Read through what you have written and underline any phrases or words that seem to point to what is ruling your heart in that situation. (i.e. fear, anger, peace, hopelessness, despair, pride.) ***Then ask yourself the following questions:***

How have I responded in this situation to avoid what is Death to me?
What is ruling my heart in this situation?
What is the truth about this experience?
What does God want to teach me through this situation?

In your small group this week be prepared to share what is Life and Death to you and what God taught you through this assignment.

It's been hard work. Thanks for taking the journey.

Next Assignment: Principle Four, Assignment Three, page 96

PRINCIPLE FOUR

We seek accountability and growth in our character as children of God.

During the last years of our marriage I became desperate for intimate relationships. I had a close friend who was a pastor and another man in my church whom I confided in on a regular basis, but I also wanted to be involved with other people who were experiencing life with a spouse struggling with sexual addiction. I got involved with New Creation Ministries in Fresno, California, and began participating in their spouse's group. It was a courageous step for me because I joined the group knowing that I would probably be the only male.

In that room full of women I found people who understood my pain and understood my weaknesses. We talked about our dependence on our spouses and how to break free from codependent patterns of relating. We kept each other accountable for boundaries we needed to set to protect ourselves and other ways we needed to take care of ourselves. For me what that looked like was joining a gym and exercising regularly, seeing my counselor on a weekly basis, taking medicine for depression, and joining a divorce-recovery group when my marriage ended. My relationships with people in my town and in group were crucial for the changes I needed to make in my life. –Norm

---

One of my most challenging struggles during the initial months of my journey was overcoming my unhealthy ways of coping with pain and conflict. It had always been my pattern to become silent and withdraw when I was angry or sad, and I tended to get stuck in feelings of hopelessness.

The women in my group soon began to understand my struggle as they got to know me, and they would invite me to talk about my pain instead of withdrawing into it. I really needed them to help me change. I was powerless over the ways I chose to cope. The community of my group was my ticket out of the spiral of hopelessness I consistently found myself in. They could help me do what I could not do alone. As I invited others to share my pain, I found relief and healing and change.—Deb

Accountability is an integral part of the healing journey. In fact, I would say to you that your healing and growth are dependent on your willingness to make yourself accountable to other safe people. That's especially true during these initial months of recovery.

Think about it this way, after a trauma in which your body is injured in some way, you stay closely accountable to a doctor so that he can monitor your healing and recovery. He wants to make sure that he deals promptly with any complications that arise and also gives you medical advice on how best to promote the healing of your body. But even when the wounds are healed, you still check in with your doctor once a year for your annual physical.

And so it is with us. During the initial months of our recovery, we need to stay closely connected and accountable to others on the journey in order to heal well and to learn how to help our emotions and spirits heal from the trauma of sexual betrayal. Our safe friends will also be able to help us see pitfalls along the way that will impede our progress or result in more injury to our souls. Staying accountable is good for our health!

But just what does "being accountable" mean? What do you think?

In the financial world, accounting is all about showing where and how money is used. In the world of relationships, being accountable is focused on exposing our thoughts and behaviors to others so that we can change. We learned in Principle Three that we are to confess our sins and weaknesses to a safe group of spiritual people. Accountability goes one step further. We not only express our sins and weaknesses, we talk about our desires, our thought-life, our hopes and our dreams. In so doing our goal is to allow others to see the real us and to support us as we make wise decisions that help us heal and grow. **Being accountable is all about pursuing change through the powerful influence and support of authentic relationships.**

Let's explore for a few moments what we are to be accountable for in our small groups every week.

Our Failures and our Thoughts about Our Failures

We need to let our fellow journeyers know about our struggles—uncontrolled rages, shopping binges, out-of-control eating, obsession with our physical appearance, flirting with others of the opposite sex, dependent relationships, etc. It's a Biblical principle we've already talked about: "Confess your sins to each other and pray for each other so that you may be healed" (James 5:16 NIV). Just as important as acknowledging our failures, however, is talking about what we think and feel about our failures.

Suppose Sally struggles with raging at her husband whenever he makes any kind of mistake. She admits that she feels powerful and in control when she's angry, and she's been telling herself that she has a right to rage considering all the stuff he's put her through. As Sally exposes these thoughts and feelings to the group, her fellow journeyers will be able to ask her what she is trying to avoid as she rages and explore her feelings of entitlement. This gives Sally a chance to see beyond her behaviors to deeper places in her heart in need of transformation and healing. She can then ask the group to hold her accountable for the way she behaves when she is angry as well as time she needs to invest with God and/or a counselor in looking beneath her anger.

Our Successes and Our Thoughts about our Successes

Group is also about rejoicing with one another. Emotional and spiritual community is built when other journeyers are able to see the fruits of the time they have invested in relating to you, praying with you, and praying for you. Just like with our failures, our thoughts about our successes tell us a great deal about what we truly believe.

Let's say Dan has been asking the group to hold him accountable for spending time relating to his son instead of zoning out in front of the TV. His commitment to relationship has resulted in two significantly emotional times with his son in which they both felt more connected than they ever have before. As Dan shares the good news in group he comments that he wishes he and his father would have been able to connect like he and his son did this week. He also reports that he and his son have made a plan to check in with each other each day before either of them get involved in other activities. The group can now encourage Dan's initiative in planning times for future intimate connections with his son and also offer their support to keep him accountable for that plan. Other journeyers might ask Dan more about his relationship with his dad and help him to uncover some unhealed wounds that need to be addressed. As Dan is accountable not only for his successes but also for his thoughts, he has a chance to see himself maturing and to also see areas that still need the Father's touch.

Our Hurts and Our Fears

Sometimes we just need someone to grieve with us. "Rejoice with those who rejoice; mourn with those who mourn," the Bible tells us (Romans 12:15 NIV). When we are grieving, there is something about just being with others who love us that is healing to our souls. So, if you are hurting, your L.I.F.E. group is a safe place to talk about the losses you have experienced and how they are impacting you.

Always connected to our losses are fears—fears of our own inadequacy, of losing more, of being hurt again. And when we are afraid, we react. We may become immobilized, we may run away, or we may raise our fists to fight. Exploring your losses and your fears with your group will help you better understand what is going on inside of you and give you an opportunity to lay down all of the yucky stuff at the feet of our Faithful One. God won't make all of your pain and fear go away, but He will help you to see it through His perspective and deal with it in a healthy way.

Our Desires

When we get down to the core of who we are, we will always find a desire behind our thoughts and behavior. Desires drive our lives—often in a sinful direction—so exposing them to others is crucial for walking well on the journey. It is not that our desires in themselves are sinful. We desire a faithful spouse who loves and cherishes us. We want our kids to be obedient, productive members of society. Our greatest hope is that we and those we love will be safe and secure, healthy and mature in all different areas of life. God has many of these same desires for us.

But the problem with our desires is that they tend to morph into something ugly and sinful. Paul David Tripp in his book, *Instruments in the Redeemer's Hands,* talks about how our desires morph into demands. He describes a demand as the closing of our fists over a desire. These demands then become perceived needs. Perceived needs morph into expectations. When these expectations are not met, then we become disappointed with others and actually punish them in some way.[v]

Let me illustrate. Brian desperately wants his wife to love and desire him. It's a good desire, created by God—a reflection in us of His desire for us to faithfully love Him. Unfortunately Angie constantly flirts with other men and pursues them sexually. After the first affair, Brian was crushed. In his heart he blamed himself for not being adequate. Those feelings of inadequacy hurt so much that he made an inner vow to get Angie's love, whatever it took. Although Brian did not realize it, his desire for a loving wife had just morphed into a demand—"I must have her love." That thought was quickly followed by, "I love her so much. I can't live without her. I need her to love me." Over the years, Brian has sacrificed much of himself and become a very angry and resentful man as Angie has failed him. He's angry at God too because God let him marry her and won't fix her. On a particularly bad day he notices an attractive woman sitting alone at his favorite coffee shop. The thought comes, "I'll make her pay. She's going to see what it feels like." Now Brian has gone from a single, God-honoring desire to sinful rebellion. See how it happens?

When we share our desires in the context of a safe group of people, others can help us keep holding our desires with open hands and show us when we have closed our fist over them. If we are to walk this journey with grace and truth, the only way we can keep from getting stuck along the way is to be accountable for our thoughts, feelings, and behaviors to others. Are you ready for some homework?

Assignment One - Becoming Accountable for What Needs to Change in My Life

In your first assignment of Principle 3, you made a list of sinful behaviors that God showed you were interfering with an intimate relationship with Him. I asked you to confess these sins to members of your small group and to share the thoughts and desires behind them if you felt safe to do so. Today, I want to take that assignment to a deeper level.

Begin by spending time with the Lord. Review the sinful attitudes and behaviors he showed you in the first assignment of Principle 3. Ask Him if there are other things He would like for you to add to your list.

As you read over your list, ask yourself the following questions and record your answers in your journal:

- On this list, I am most ashamed of ____________ because…
- The sins I habitually repeat in spite of my best efforts to change are…
- When I think about these sinful behaviors and attitudes in my life I feel…
- The sin(s) I have never confessed to anyone is…

Now in your journal write the following sentence in big, bold letters:

I NEED TO CHANGE, BUT I CAN'T DO IT ALONE.

Ask the Father to give you the courage to invite others to keep you accountable as you pursue change. In your small group this week, share at least one of your sinful behaviors or attitude. Tell the group members what you are thinking and feeling about the sin, and ask them to hold you accountable this week as you seek to change your behavior.

(For example, let's say that God has showed you that you are dependent on the approval of others and can never say no when people ask you to do something—and when you do say no on rare occasions, you lie to make yourself look better. You confess this struggle to the group and tell them your new boundary is to consider requests before making an emotional decision. You know you will need help sorting through what you really want to do in a situation, so you ask two or three group members to be available for you to call when a situation arises. When Dorothy Do-right calls from church to ask for your help at a church social later that week, you tell her you'll consider her request and get back with her. Then you call a friend from group with whom you can talk about the decision. Your friend can help you sift through what you want to do and what you feel pressured to do by your own fears or desires. This is one way to make yourself accountable.)

You are doing great! I'm so excited about the ways you are growing and changing.

Next Assignment: Principle Five, page 102

Assignment Two - My Accountability Plan

Welcome back to Principle Four. Let's review:

We seek accountability and growth in our character as children of God.

In our first lesson on this principle we focused on being accountable for our thoughts, feelings, desires, and behaviors in authentic relationships with others in order to change behaviors and attitudes which are not characteristic of children of God. We practiced being real about our sins and weaknesses in our small groups and asking others to hold us accountable for the changes we need to make.

Let's talk about change for a minute. When we discuss things we need to change in order to grow in our character as God's children, I want you to think in terms of attitudes and behaviors that need to be avoided as well as attitudes and behaviors that need to be added to our lives. Dr. Mark Laaser calls these "bottom line" and "top line" behaviors. **Bottom line behaviors** *describe conduct we need to avoid*, and **top line behaviors** *describe healthy choices we need to make in our lives on a daily basis*.[vi]

Very often in recovery we focus on the bad things we are doing because these behaviors generate so much shame and pain. Actually, the guilt and sorrow you feel when you behave in sinful ways is a very good sign in your life. It shows that you are God's child and that His Spirit is alive and active in you—seeking to transform you more and more into God's image. So, often we have great motivation to try to change the sinful behaviors in our lives, but we neglect healthy behaviors that enable us to face life with God's heart and mind and to grow up in Him. Some of them are very simple things like getting enough rest, eating a balanced, healthy diet, exercising, playing with your kids or family members, spending time alone with God each day. Others are choices that require more investment in time and energy—developing and maintaining authentic relationships, carving out time to get to know God and yourself at a deeper level, committing yourself to compassionate and consistent intercession for others, being a voice of grace and truth in the lives of others on the journey.

And when we talk about accountability, we not only need to be accountable for the things we need to take out of our lives but also for the things we need to put in. In my own life, I had so neglected myself in my effort to placate and please my husband that I was unhealthy in every area of my life. I struggled with secret sins that kept me bound in my relationship with God and isolated from others, I ate poorly, I didn't exercise, I was constantly tired, I had no true friends, and I didn't even know what I liked anymore. My accountability process started with me confessing my sinful behaviors to those I trusted and grew to include choices I needed to make to get my life back in balance and growing towards Christ-likeness.

I admit, sometimes it is overwhelming. I'm not a great multi-tasker like many women are. I tend to get focused on one thing and let the other things of life fall by the wayside. It's a running joke in my family that I can't do laundry and chew gum at the same time. I have to have a "laundry day" where I am focused just on the task of doing laundry. So, knowing my weaknesses, I ask for help. When I'm feeling overwhelmed with all that I have to do, I call one of my closest friends, a fellow group member. I ask her to hold me accountable for what I need to do to take care of myself and also for what I need to avoid–usually some mental escape like looking at a catalog or decorating the guest room in my mind. Often, just exposing my struggles to my friends gives me the courage to make the

right choices because I feel less alone. I know they are standing with me, loving me and praying for me. I've said it before, and I'll say it again. Authentic relationships have changed my life.
So, with all of this in mind, today you are going to develop an accountability plan for all that God is showing you needs to change in your life—both the behaviors you need to avoid and those you need to add. But be careful! This is not some kind of divine to-do list that you must accomplish in order to earn God's love or approval or to avoid his displeasure and condemnation. Rather, these are the places in your heart God wants to transform by His grace and power through your surrender and participation. The journey is not about perfection. It's about persistence and perseverance. We won't be made complete until we cross the finish line. What we are trying to do is to walk well—with enough energy to give back to others and without all the weights and stumbling blocks that keep tripping us up.

One more word before I give you the assignment. You will need at least two people in your life (of your same gender) with whom you can be accountable. They should be people who have walked at least the same distance as you have on the journey and people with whom you feel safe to share the real you, warts and all. I say at least two people because accountability is most effective when more than one pair of eyes is watching you walk. One person may not be available when you need him/her. One person may get distracted and not see you stumble. But when two or more people are walking with you, one of them is sure to see when you are struggling. Also, because I have been prone to become involved in dependent relationships with other women during my life, it is much easier for me to have appropriate boundaries and avoid unhealthy dependencies when I am consistently relating to a group of women authentically.

I would also add that it would be helpful for you to have someone in a mentoring role in your life, especially during your first leg of the journey. AA calls these kinds of people "sponsors." The idea is that you are in relationship with someone who has walked farther than you and can help you see where you are going as well as pitfalls you may encounter along the way. I realize that it may be difficult for you to find a person who shares your life experience and is in a position to walk with you in a mentoring relationship. Sometimes a professional counselor can fill that role for you for a time. Often, God will place a person in your life for a season to help you walk through a particular section of the journey. If you can't think of anyone who is in a position to mentor you at this time, just keep your spiritual eyes and ears open, and ask the Father to send someone to fill that role in your life. He knows your needs, and He will be faithful in His time.

I've talked enough. It's time for us to get to the homework. Are you excited?

I'm excited for you because I know how much God is going to impact your life through these accountable relationships. Let's get started.

In your journal write the heading, "<u>My Accountability Plan</u>."

Begin by making a list of <u>Behaviors I Need to Avoid</u>. ***(When you have finished your list, choose one or two that you sense God most wants to deal with in your life right now. Put a star by this/these behaviors.)***

When you have completed that list, record daily <u>Choices I Need to Make</u>. ***(Again, brainstorm a complete list and write down what the Father brings to your mind, Then choose one or two choices that you feel God most wants you to make right now. Put a star by this/these choices.)***

Then write the heading <u>My Accountability Partners</u>. ***List at least two people with whom you feel safe to be accountable.*** (It might be helpful to list as many as five or six in case they cannot enter into this accountable relationship with you for some reason.)

During this week, call the people you have listed and ask them if they would be willing to keep you accountable on a regular basis. (I check in with my accountability partners at least once a week.)

Now write the questions that your accountability partners need to ask you during your weekly check-in. *(Focus on the one or two behaviors you want to avoid and choices you need to make you put a star by earlier.)* In my life, I have instructed my accountability people to ask me about my sugar intake, about how much time I have spent looking at catalogs or engaging in mental escape behaviors, and about how I am dealing with my tendency to seek out approval from men I admire and respect. They also know to ask me about ways I am taking care of myself and what healthy choices I am making to ensure that I have emotional, physical, and spiritual energy to accomplish what God sets before me to do.

Try to write your questions in an open-ended way so that when you respond to them your accountability partners will get the big picture of what is going on in your heart and life. (For example, instead of writing the question "Did you use TV inappropriately this week?" write the question, "How much time did you spend escaping by watching TV, and what were you feeling at those times?")

Lastly, think through your plan, should you find yourself in a situation in which you are tempted to behave sinfully. In your journal, write the heading <u>My Plan When I Am Triggered/Tempted.</u> ***List the actions you will take to avoid behaving sinfully.*** (For instance, I call my accountability partners when I am feeling overwhelmed and a catalog arrives in the mail. I know that when I am feeling anxious and overwhelmed, my greatest temptation is to escape into a world that I can control and keep perfectly clean and organized.)

Your final task is to make a copy of everything you've written for your accountability partners and to give it to them in a face-to-face time of relating. Talk with them about any fears or shame you are experiencing, and take time to pray together.

You've done a lot of challenging work. I'm proud of your diligence and effort.

Next Assignment: Principle Five, Assignment Two, page 106

Assignment Three - The Past Meets the Present: Idols of My Heart

You've done a lot of hard work to get to this point. I'm proud of you and excited about what God is doing in your heart and life. Let's review Principle Four one last time.

We seek accountability and growth in our character as children of God.

Let's check in for a minute. ***How have you grown since the last time we studied this principle together?***

How are your intimate relationships with others—specifically in your small group? Are you pursuing intimacy? How?

I pray you are able to see the great transformation taking place in your life and heart regardless of what your marriage or other life circumstances look like. Today we are going to be doing more stretching and growing, stuff centered around our own growth and maturity as believers on the journey. Are you ready?

First, tell me what you think about when I say the word, idol.

For a long time when I heard the word idol I pictured some figure carved in wood or sculpted in stone or metal. My mind went back to the Old Testament days and to foreign lands where idols adorned temples and religious sites. It was hard for me to think about idolatry in my own heart and life because I didn't bow down to any image or icon. I worshipped the one true God—or so I believed.

There is a different kind of idol, though—an unseen idol—an idol of the heart. And unfortunately, my heart was full of them. You see, an idol is anything we turn to other than God for comfort, love, security, safety, significance, or acceptance. Think about your life. What do you do when you are scared? When you are sad? When you are lonely? When you feel rejected?

So often, instead of seeking out an intimate time of closeness with God when we are feeling these things, we gorge ourselves on chocolate, or stay late at the office working overtime, or masturbate, or fantasize. We may zone out in front of the TV, or lose ourselves in a good book, or find someone who needs us in some way. The list goes on and on. Anything, any behavior, any person can become an idol in our lives. It is all a matter of the heart.

As you walk in recovery and read books about addiction you may come upon the phrase "coping strategies" or "ways of coping." Many psychologists would describe our compulsive TV watching, eating, exercising, working, etc. as ways we cope with our emotional pain and emptiness. But I prefer to call all of these behaviors what they really are in the eyes of God—idols of the heart. As spouses we often see our mate's sexual behaviors as so much worse than our sinful choices. But to God, sin is sin. We and our spouses have done the same thing—just in different ways. True, the consequences of sexual sin are greater than the consequences of eating a pan of brownies in one sitting, but God sees our hearts more than He sees our behaviors. It's a hard pill to swallow, but our idolatry is just as sinful as our spouses'. As I have walked my own journey and talked with other spouses along the way, I've found some common idols of the heart many of us struggle with. They are as follows:

Idol #1—Relationships

This is probably the most common idol among spouses of addicts. We become dependent on others for love, significance, and security, and in the process God gets bumped off the throne of our hearts. Instead of allowing Him to meet our needs, we spend most of our time placating and pleasing and controlling and manipulating other people in order to get our needs met through them. We've talked about this idol already by a different name—codependence or co-addiction.

Idolatrous relationships are really self-centered and self-serving. We are using others to get our needs met. A good sign that you are in an idolatrous relationship with someone is that your happiness and serenity is based on how the other person is doing. If he/she is behaving in ways that make you feel loved and secure, you have a great day. But if the other person betrays you or acts in ways that make you feel alone and afraid, you experience what feels like death to you. When we are addicted to—a.k.a. worshipping—another person and what we think that person can and should give to us, we live in fear of what he/she can take away. Instead of experiencing all of the things we so desperately crave, we end up in a prison of our own making, depending on someone who has no power to meet our needs.

Idol #2—Children

Our relationship with our children can become idolatrous when we live for their happiness, when we depend on their approval or respect to meet our own needs, when we live vicariously through them, or when we depend on them to meet emotional needs our spouse should be meeting. When we live for our children's happiness we tend to be so focused on them that our other relationships are neglected. All of our energy goes into trying to meet our children's needs and prevent any pain from happening in their lives—an agenda, by the way, that will result in entitled, immature teenagers and adults. Our children's happiness becomes more important than God's happiness.

Sometimes we come to depend on our children's love or respect to meet our needs for acceptance and significance. If you struggle with this idolatry you may have difficulty setting boundaries with your children because you fear them disliking or hating you. You may be very strict and rules-oriented with your kids, demanding obedience or else. Parents who are more rules-oriented than relationship-oriented are often depending on their children's behavior to prove to the world that they are competent and adequate parents.

Other times our idolatry takes the form of trying to live vicariously through our kids' lives. We feel successful if they are successful and feel like a failure if they fail. A parent-child relationship characterized by this dynamic is marked by tremendous pressure. Your children feel great pressure to perform perfectly, and you live in constant anxiety about whether or not they will succeed.

Finally, a very abusive form of idolatry takes place when we depend on a child to meet our emotional needs. No child should be called on to support us when we are lonely or afraid. No child should be put in the position of protecting us from an abusive spouse or "helping" us catch our spouse betraying us in some way. We are called to be parents and nurturers—not needy victims. Our job is to meet the needs of our children—not to have our needs met by them. We need to be honest about our feelings and the reality of our marriage, but we must always bear in mind that we are the grown-ups and that our children need to remain children.

Idol #3—Work

Work is such an easy idol to worship. When we excel and succeed in the world, others are quick to affirm us and brag on our talents and competence. We feel so significant and valuable. And it's such a temptation to invest more time and energy into work where we get so many positive strokes than in a relationship that is imperfect and often less than positive. We begin to live for the affirmation and "atta-boys" from others instead of living for the agenda of our Lord.

Idol #4—Ministry or Religious Service

This is the same idol of the heart we talked about with work but with a religious twist. There is always the temptation to find life in the service rather than the Servant. And it's a very subtle idolatry because we think we are working for God instead of trying to meet our own needs. Those of us who worship the idol of ministry often live double lives, struggling with some secret sin or compulsion while doing lots of good works hoping to balance out the bad stuff in our hearts. We also tend to get angry or resentful when people don't notice our work and sacrifice, and we feel like a "nobody" apart from our ministry. Our entire identity is wrapped up in what we do, our job title, instead of whose we are. One last symptom of this idol worship is our inability to be authentic with others about what is really going on inside of us. Ministers who serve freely always pursue intimacy with other believers.

Idol #5—Exercise/Physical Fitness/Body Image

When our external appearance and the way others perceive us becomes the focus of our lives, we are worshipping at the altar of this particular idol. Some of us exercise compulsively, diet excessively, spend lots of money on cosmetics, physical enhancements, or plastic surgery—all so that we can be physically attractive. Instead of worrying about our hearts, we make our outsides look better. It's not sinful to exercise and eat healthy for the purpose of caring for the body God has given us. But we cross the line when it becomes more important to look good physically than to walk in intimate relationship with God and others. God cares nothing about your physical appearance. He loves your insides. He loves you.

Idol #6—Imagination, Fantasy, and Other Ways to Escape from Reality

I know what this idolatry looks like very well. It was a part of my life for a long time as I escaped the pain of my marriage. Fantasy alters our mood. In a few moments we can forget all about our unfaithful spouse and be in the arms of a person who loves us and never betrays our trust. And because just imagining a different life can make us feel better, fantasy is very addictive. Even when our fantasies are not sexual in nature, we can get a tremendous sense of relief from just decorating a room in our mind or dreaming about a significant promotion at work.

Also included in this idolatry are behaviors which don't necessarily seem sinful but help us escape from the often painful reality of our lives—zoning out in front of the TV for hours at a time, immersing ourselves in a novel, spending hours on the internet, etc. Again, balance is key. We all need down time, but we must learn to differentiate between restful times that help us recharge and sinful coping strategies that keep us isolated from God and others. In my opinion, the most negative thing about this particular idol is that when we are fantasizing or mentally escaping in other ways, we are not living in reality and therefore we are missing out on healing relationships.

Idol #7—Food

Food is a huge idol in the lives of many, including myself. We use food to nurture ourselves, eating when we're not hungry, eating when we sad or lonely or tired. We can also use food to keep a sense of control in our lives—rigidly controlling what we eat in order to maintain a certain body image or intentionally gaining weight to protect us from those who might hurt us physically or emotionally. The goal is to have a right relationship with food—eating for the health and well-being of your body and not to meet the emotional needs of your soul.

Idol #8—Substances

Most of us are very aware of the way people have chosen to use substances to deal with the pain and disappointments of life. When we use narcotics, alcohol, over the counter medicines, pain killers, sleeping pills, caffeine, or nicotine to numb out or alter our mood, we are worshipping at the altar of Escape. We need to be very careful about becoming dependent on something created rather than depending on the Creator for the needs of our souls.

With that said, I do want to be very clear that those of us who have physiological conditions that require certain drugs and chemicals for emotional and/or physical health are not sinning. Again, it is a heart matter. What we take into our bodies should help us connect in intimate relationship with God and others. We cannot connect with Him if we are shut down in an acute or chronic depression. So, there are times when substances actually help us on the journey. What we should guard against are substances that help us escape from reality and the intimate relationship with God and others that we so desperately need.

Idol #9—Shopping

This is a big idol, particularly for female spouses. Many of us use shopping as an escape from the painful reality of life. We feel powerful and capable when we shop. We feel like we have choices, and that gives us a sense of control. Obviously, we do need to shop for groceries and other items, so the key is to have a balanced heart. If your heart is out of whack, you will shop and buy things you don't need or that are not in the budget. You may neglect your responsibilities at home because you are shopping instead of attending to necessary tasks. You might lie about where you've been or how much money you've spent. Much of your time might be spent looking through ads/catalogs, fantasizing about what you would like to buy. And you might isolate yourself from others when you shop, finding excuses to go shopping instead of relating to other people.

Idol #10—Sex

I know. It's your spouse who struggles with the idol of sex. Before you get defensive though, see if you can relate to any of these idolatrous beliefs and behaviors:

You may believe sex equals intimacy so your marriage centers on sex rather than emotional and spiritual oneness. You resolve conflicts by having sex, feel rejected when your spouse is not sexual with you, have sex when you really don't want to, and become dependent on a sexual relationship for feelings of love and acceptance.

Being sexual might feel like "death" to you because sex is associated with pain or shame. You may become unable to give or receive sexually. Or you may pursue sex because you only feel accepted when you are sexual. Both obsessions with sex—either avoiding it or pursuing it—take your focus away from God's agenda for you because you are trying to meet your needs apart from Him. You may masturbate to soothe or nurture yourself. It's not just our spouses who struggle with this behavior. We can become addicted to the hormones released during sexual arousal and climax and short-circuit intimacy by being sexual with ourselves. I personally struggled with masturbation a great deal, especially during the time when Troy was acting out and rejecting me sexually. Most often my masturbation was connected to a romantic fantasy in which I was loved and cherished and desired. Over time, however, masturbation became a way for me to comfort myself when I was feeling unloved and alone.

You may dress provocatively (as a female) to get male attention and affirmation. It's mostly about power and control, but we are also hungering for love and acceptance when this is our struggle. When we are intentionally trying to catch a man's eye, we are trying to meet our needs through a person instead of the Lover of our Souls.

You may become a hero (as a male) to get female attention and affirmation. There is nothing quite so heady as being someone's knight in shining armor. It's about significance, adequacy, and competence, and it's a subtle idolatry because it looks so good and gentlemanly. Again, kindness is good, but examine your heart and be sure that you are not simply seeking to get your own needs met by rescuing the damsel in distress.

You may use sex to control or manipulate your spouse. If you have withheld sex to punish your spouse or offered sex, knowing that you would be rewarded in some way, you have been guilty of this form of idolatry. When we use sex to get our way, God is certainly not on the throne of our hearts. There are times when it is wise and good to disconnect from our spouses sexually. However, sex used as a power tool never promotes intimacy or relationship.

You may be sexual with others outside of your marriage. Some of us have engaged in sexual behaviors with others in order to punish our unfaithful spouses and to have our revenge. Others of us, like our spouses, believe that sex is our greatest need and the only way we can find love and acceptance. Freedom comes when we begin to trust God with our spouses and when we begin to see that knowing God is our greatest need.

Are you identifying any idols in your own heart through our study today? Let's take some time to sift and sort.

Think about all of the idols we have talked about today. Did you see your own heart described anywhere? In your journal write down any idols you have worshipped in your heart, and be specific about how you have used these people, things, or behaviors to meet needs only God can fill. (For example, if you write down "food" as an idol in your life, explain how you use food illegitimately—i.e. I eat sweets when I am feeling lonely or sad.)

When you are finished making your list, in your journal or on a separate piece of paper draw an altar—whatever you think one looks like. Then on the altar, draw symbols that represent the idols you have been depending on in your heart.

Now it's time to pray. ***Invite the Father to look at your drawing and tell Him about each of the idols you've discovered in your heart. Ask Him to forgive you for depending on other people and things instead of turning to Him. Talk to Him about any difficulties you have trusting Him, and ask Him to help you see your own heart clearly.***

Ask the Father which idolatry He most wants to deal with in your life right now. Write down His answer in your journal.

Sex addicts entering recovery are asked to abstain from any sexual activity for 90 days. This ninety-day period is a time when their bodies can de-tox from their dependence on the chemicals released during sexual climax and a time when they can emotionally begin to tear down the false belief in their hearts that sex is their greatest need. If you are married to a sex addict in recovery, you are probably already aware of the 90-day abstinence contract and understand why it is so important for healing.

Today, we are going to ask you to make a similar commitment—a 90-day fast from whatever coping strategy (a.k.a. idol) God has put His finger on in your heart. When I challenged the ladies in my group with this idea, God was showing me how much I depended on sugar for comfort and an extra burst of energy when I felt tired. So I fasted from all refined sugars for 90 days. It was a life-changing experience for me. Perhaps you struggle with zoning out in front of the TV or masturbating or flirting or working incessantly or shopping or reading romantic novels. Whatever it is that you tend to do apart from God when you are feeling lonely, afraid, unloved, or insignificant, I am asking you to lay it aside for 90 days.

In group this week, you will have two things to share. First, share your drawing with your small group and talk to your friends about the idols you discovered in your heart. Second, tell your group members what you will be fasting from for 90 days and have them witness the contract below.

I, ____________________, am choosing to fast from ____________________ for 90 days in order to begin depending on God for my deepest needs.

Date: ________________ Signed: ______________________________________

Witnessed by: ____

Next Assignment: Principle Five, Assignment Three, page 111

PRINCIPLE FIVE

We explore the wounds from our pasts, acknowledge our sinful choices in response to those hurts, and allow God to transform and heal our hearts.

I know now that I just shut down emotionally. We had been married about ten years when my mother died. Mom and I were very close—too close, really. I was emotionally dependent on her support. And when she was gone, I didn't know what to do with the pain. So I focused all of my energy on work. I would be gone all week and come home exhausted on the weekends. My wife was running the house and raising our kids single-handedly. I had nothing to give her emotionally, and I know she felt abandoned—just like she did when her father died when she was thirteen. To be honest, I know my unhealthy and sinful way of dealing with pain was the catalyst for my wife's first affair. Both of us were wounded, but neither of us understood the depths of our brokenness. One of the things I had to do was to ask my wife to forgive me for the way I shut her and everyone else out of my life during that time in my life. –Norm

---

I walked off of the plane and into his arms. "I forgive you, Troy. Everything is going to be okay." Troy looked overwhelmed. He was hugging our daughter and looking at his new son for the first time. All I wanted was for us to be okay.

At that point in my journey I was still numb. I had felt no anger towards my husband or his sin, and I had only begun to grieve. Over the next few weeks and months as Troy disclosed all that he had done and I began to fully understand what all we had lost, I realized that my forgiveness had not been forgiveness at all. Instead it was a desperate attempt to make Troy love me and to save our marriage. I hadn't even considered the debt I was forgiving when I told him I forgave him. And I was angry, hurt to my core, broken, and crushed.

And so the process of forgiveness began for me. I learned the whole truth. I grieved the losses. And then, one by one, I let them go. –Melissa

As we work through Principle Five, we will be focusing on three actions: exploring the wounds from our pasts, acknowledging any sinful choices in response to those hurts, and allowing God to transform and heal our hearts. I want us to start today with the most recent wound we've experienced—the betrayal of our spouse.

How did you respond when you discovered your spouse had been engaging in sexual behaviors outside of your relationship?

Some of us went ballistic—breaking things and raging at our spouse. Others of us ignored the pain and told our spouse and ourselves that everything would be okay. Hopefully a few of us were authentic about our pain and yet healthy in the way we expressed it. Of course, some of us ran away from the pain altogether. And others of us never had a chance to express our feelings because our spouse abandoned the relationship.

No matter how you found out about your spouse's struggle with sexual addiction and no matter how you responded, at some point on your journey you will need to deal with the issue of forgiveness. Forgiveness is not really an option for believers. The Bible tells us that if we want to be in right relationship with God, then we must forgive those who wound us—and forgive them from our hearts (Matthew 18:35).

But what is forgiveness? What do you think?

In the simplest of language, **forgiveness** is *canceling a debt owed to us*. It is taking an account of outstanding charges and writing below the sum total in big red letters, **"Debt Remitted—No Payment Due."** When we forgive a person who has hurt us, we are releasing him from the debt he owes us. Forgiveness does not mean that the debt will no longer impact us or cause us pain. Forgiveness does not mean that we automatically trust our spouse again or live as if nothing ever happened. It does not necessarily mean that we will continue in a married relationship with our spouse. Forgiveness does mean that we will no longer require payment—whatever that looks like—from the one who has wounded us.

Let's talk about what requiring payment might look like. What are your ideas?

When we have not forgiven a debt, there are many ways we may exact payment from the one who has hurt us. We can withdraw from the relationship—freezing her out emotionally. We may use the offense as leverage to get things we want. We might constantly bring up our hurt and pain in an effort to remind him how much he has hurt us. We can become abusive, calling our spouse names and verbally (and/or physically) attacking him. We may abandon the relationship without any effort to reconcile. We might turn our children against our spouse. The list could go on. There are hundreds of ways we make people pay for what they have done to us.

But God calls us to walk differently as His children. Knowing how difficult it would be for us to forgive those who betray our trust, He Himself modeled what forgiveness from the heart looks like. One glimpse of the cross is all it takes for us to understand how important forgiveness is to the Father.

But how do we forgive? How do we let go of such deep hurt and betrayal? Would you use your sanctified imagination with me for a moment?

> Imagine that you and your spouse are standing in a courtroom. God is sitting in the judge's seat, and Jesus is standing in between you and your spouse. The charges have been read, and God asks your spouse one question: "How will you repay this debt?"
>
> Your spouse, looking into the eyes of God, shamefully but honestly answers in a small voice, "I can't."
>
> Then God looks at you and asks you one question: "What will you have me do to your mate?"

Write down what you would say to God.

"Very well, God says. He motions to the officials in the courtroom. They walk toward you and your spouse, but instead of taking your spouse away, they take the arm of Jesus.

"What's going on?" you ask. Your spouse looks astonished as well.

God answers, "Before this trial, your Advocate came to me and told me He wanted to pay the debt for your spouse. I agreed that whatever you asked me to do to your spouse, He would have done to Him.

Your heart is filled with a wave of grief and anger it has never known before. You begin to protest.

Then God, with tears running down His face, looks at both you and your spouse and says, "You are both free. Your advocate, My Son, has paid the debt for the sin and the cost of forgiveness. Go, and live in peace."

Stunned, you both leave the courtroom.

What would you be thinking at this point?

I have had a lot of people ask me over the years how I forgave Troy for his infidelity and verbal abuse. I always struggle to respond to that question for several reasons. First, it is tempting to bask in the approval and affirmation of people who believe I'm some great spiritual giant because I was able to forgive Troy. Second, I don't want to respond with a cliché that does not capture the reality of forgiveness. And third, the person asking me doesn't have time to listen to the list of my own sinful choices that can only be covered by the forgiving grace of God.

The reality is, though, that I was able to forgive Troy because Jesus paid the debt Troy owed me. He took all the scorn and hatred and anger and disgust I felt for Troy, all the shame, all the broken promises, all the lies. He took it all on Himself and carried it. And then He touched my face and told me how much He loved me, how valuable I was to Him. To refuse to forgive Troy would have been saying to Jesus that what He gave me was not enough.

My dear friend, if you want to be whole, there must come a time when you release your spouse from the debt he/she owes you and allow what Christ has offered on behalf of your husband or wife to be enough. It is His grace that enables us to forgive—grace given to our spouses and grace given to us.

It's time to take a look at our hearts with Him.

Assignment One - Betrayal: An Opportunity to Forgive

At the top of a new page in your journal write the heading, "The Debts My Spouse Owes Me." ***Now make a list of all of the debts your spouse accrued as a result of his/her sexual addiction. Be sure to include emotional, physical, spiritual, and relational debts.***

When you are finished, answer these questions in your journal.

- Which of these debts can be repaid in some way? (Underline them in your list.)
- How do you expect them to be paid? Be as specific as possible.
- Which of these debts can never be repaid? (Circle them in your list.)
- Right now I feel __________because __________
- I have forgiven my spouse for …
- I am still struggling to forgive my spouse for… because…
- The ways I keep making my spouse pay are…
- My desire is to…

Now ask the Father to look at the list of debts. Talk to Him about which debts you are struggling to forgive and ask Him to carry them for you. Read through the debts one by one. If you are ready to allow Christ's offer to be enough for the debt, tell Him your decision and write "Paid in Full" over that debt in your journal. End your time with the Lord by thanking Him for His grace and telling Him what His grace means to you.

In your small group this week, share what God showed you and what debts you forgave.

If you are still in relationship with your spouse, ask those in your small group if they feel it would be wise at this time for you to share this assignment with your spouse.

Next Assignment: Principle Six, page 116

Assignment Two -
Accepting Responsibility and Making Amends

We're back at Principle Five. Do you remember what is says?

We explore the wounds from our pasts, acknowledge our sinful choices in response to those hurts, and allow God to transform and heal our hearts.

Our first lesson on this principle explored the wounds caused by our spouses' sexual betrayal, the ways we have made them pay, and God's call to forgive. It was a challenging lesson, and I want to prepare you by saying that our study today may even be more difficult for you. Today we will be focusing on our failures and amends we need to make in our relationships.

Let's check in. How are you feeling about this assignment right now? (Check and explain all that apply.)

- ❑ Angry because ______________________________
- ❑ Defensive because ______________________________
- ❑ Sad because ______________________________
- ❑ Anxious because ______________________________
- ❑ Worried because ______________________________
- ❑ Guilty because ______________________________
- ❑ Ashamed because ______________________________
- ❑ Peaceful because ______________________________
- ❑ Teachable because ______________________________
- ❑ ______________ because ______________________________

Even at this point on my journey there is still something in me that bristles when someone says to me, "Let's talk about your stuff, Mel." I don't know if you are as broken as I am, but I hate to be wrong. I hate to fail. I hate to have to say, "I'm sorry that I hurt you." For me, being wrong is really scary because I fear that my failures will result in rejection. It would take me too long to walk through my past and show you where that belief came from, but suffice it to say, I am afraid to fail. Thankfully, God has been so faithful to help me see that false belief in operation and to challenge me to rest in His love in spite of my performance. (He has this way of not rescuing me from my failures so that I get a lot of practice resting in His love. Smile.)

I say all of this because I want you to realize that when we have difficulty acknowledging our failures and making amends it usually is because our failures mean more to us then just failing. For some reason, we see failure as one step away from rejection, abandonment, or insignificance. And those things feel like death to us.

Now, we can put up several fronts to hide our fear of failure. Let me list a few.

- ❑ We can exhibit a prideful attitude which says, "I can't be wrong because I've been a more responsible and better person than you have."
- ❑ We can accept all the blame put on us with an outwardly submissive appearance while inside we are seething with resentment.
- ❑ We can push all the bad away from us by blaming others and denying our failure.

- ❑ We can shirk responsibility by pleading ignorance or saying, "I didn't mean to."
- ❑ We can minimize the offense we have caused so that we feel like less of a failure.
- ❑ We can run away from relationships in which we have failed so that we don't have to face the reality of our failure.
- ❑ We can act like we haven't failed and ignore the problem until the other person forgets or lays it aside.
- ❑ We can lie or tell a half-truth in order to avoid facing our failure.
- ❑ We can compare our failures to the failures of others to make us feel less wrong or less bad.

Are you finding yourself in any of these? (Check the ways you have avoided your failures.)

I personally have used all of these methods of avoiding my failures. And it is with heartfelt compassion that I say to you my friend, if we are to grow up in Him we must learn to deal with failure by acknowledging our wrongs and making amends. It doesn't matter how others have failed. When God looks at us, He is interested in dealing with our hearts—not the hearts of our spouses.

You have already been working on confessing your sins and weaknesses to a safe group of people and allowing them to hold you accountable for your stuff. Today, we are going to take that one step further and talk about making amends. We are also going to broaden the relationships we are evaluating to include not just our spouses but also others—our children, other family members, co-workers, and friends.

And I want to remind you of something of which God often reminds me. King David was a very spiritual man who had a dynamic relationship with God. And he failed in a very big way. Do you remember how Samuel the Prophet described David in 1 Samuel 13:14? "The Lord has sought out a man after His own heart and appointed him leader of His people." The same man who had a heart like God's lived a far from perfect life, but notice how David responded when confronted with his sinful choices—"Then David said to Nathan, 'I have sinned against the Lord.' (2 Samuel 12:13 NIV)." He didn't minimize or deny or plead ignorance or compare his sin to that of others. He simply acknowledged what he had done. Although God took the life of David's son to show the world that David's sin had grieved Him, the beautiful thing about the story is the way God redeemed David's sin. He used the woman David took unlawfully to bear a son named Solomon who would become the wisest and wealthiest king of Israel's history and who would eventually build the temple of God.

You see, when we humbly acknowledge our mistakes and sins, God uses our failures for our good and His glory. There is nothing we can do in this life that God can't redeem in some way if we are willing to own our failures and walk with Him through them.

Do you believe that?

Acknowledging our failures and our sinful choices is an absolutely essential part of growing up in Christ. Making amends where we are able is an absolutely essential part of growing relationally with others.

Let's talk about making amends for a moment. ***What does the phrase "making amends" mean to you?***

The root word "mend" in the word "amends" gives us a clue into its meaning. When we make **amends** we *try to correct or repair damage or hurt we have caused by our words and behaviors.* Making amends is not about getting things back to normal or keeping peace. On the contrary, it is about relating authentically to those we love and paying outstanding debts freely from a sincere heart.

There are some debts, of course, that we cannot repay. We cannot remove the pain and hurt of words said in anger. We cannot change our past choices and the consequences we and our loved ones have experienced as a result of them. And we cannot restore a shattered dream.

We can, however, choose to take responsibility for our choices and set our faces in the direction of grace and truth from now on. We can use our words to build relationships instead of tearing them down. We can become aware of how our choices are impacting those we love and relate to them more lovingly and honestly. And we can become a part of a new dream.

One of my greatest failures in my relationship with Troy was my dishonesty with him. I was afraid of his anger and losing his love, and I lied all the time to myself and to him to keep myself from experiencing his rejection. My dishonesty set up a very unhealthy dynamic in our marriage. Troy would get angry about something, and I would minimize or excuse or justify or deny that I had failed. His anger would escalate as he felt unheard and disrespected, and he would become verbally abusive. I would cry or run away from his presence, and he would leave feeling frustrated and discouraged. I constantly felt unloved. He constantly felt disrespected. We were on an infinity loop of emotional pain and hopelessness. Added to that were all of the acting out behaviors both of us were doing to numb our pain. Troy was acting out sexually with himself and other people. I was escaping into a world of fantasy—decorating houses in my mind and weaving tales of romance and passion in which I was loved and desired. Both of us were using our ministry as missionaries to gain some sense of significance and value. Instead of serving others from the fullness of Christ in us, we were serving others from our neediness. Our reality was agonizingly painful.

When we began working on our stuff and got through the grief of all the sexual betrayal and loss resulting from Troy's sexual addiction, we still found ourselves in this cycle of conflict—much to our dismay. It was then that I began to realize my part in it all, how much my dishonesty had impacted our relationship. I apologized to Troy and committed to turn my face toward truth, even when I was afraid of his rejection. In the years we've been walking in recovery together, I have struggled to be honest, at times, and have had to own my dishonesty with Troy. My making amends for this pattern of self-protective lying in our relationship will probably be a life-long process of speaking as truthfully as I can so that Troy can continue to grow to trust that my words are reflecting what is truly in my heart.

Some of us, on the other hand, don't struggle with being truthful. We protect ourselves by raging and using our words to condemn others and inflict pain. It is true that some of what we are saying is an honest expression of our hearts. It is also true that we abuse a great gift God has given us. Our words carry the power of life and death, you know. And many of us bombard others with more words of death than words of life. If you have acted on your feelings in sinful ways, making amends will involve both apology and change.

And one more word before we get to the homework. Sometimes the most overlooked offenses are towards our children. Because you have power in your relationship with your children, they will often internalize offenses instead of voicing their hurts. I make it a point to check in with my kids every few weeks to see if I have hurt them in some way, to understand if they are harboring anger or resentment towards me.

Sometimes I am astounded by their answers. "Mommy, when you talked about what I did to Mrs. Becky, you embarrassed me. I wanted to go hide." OUCH! "Mommy, I felt so unloved when you didn't let me help you in the kitchen. I felt like I wasn't good enough for you." Double OUCH!

I try to keep a short account of debts with my kids. I don't want them to harbor secret resentments or hurts that in my ignorance I don't resolve and, in their brokenness, become a life-dominating pattern of relating as they grow. I am very serious about breaking the cycle of dysfunction and unhealthiness Troy and I brought into our marriage.

I hope you are understanding the importance of owning your failures and making amends. It's that time again. Let's practice what we're learning.

Let's start by connecting with God. Complete the following sentences in your journal as a prayer to Him.

Father, as I think about owning my failures and making amends I feel...
My fear is that...
But I want to trust Your...
Help me to see myself clearly and to have the courage to face my failures. I want to...
Thank You for...
I love You.

As you spend time with the Lord, write down failures that you know have impacted your relationship with your spouse and other people in your life. (You made a list of some of those failures in Principle 3, Assignment 1.)

For each failure, answer the following questions:

- Have I acknowledged my failure in this relationship?
- Have I apologized?
- Have I made amends as best I know how?
- If I have not made amends, what can I do to repair the hurt I've caused?

The next part of the assignment involves some research. ***If you are at a safe point in your relationship with your spouse, ask him/her in what ways things you have done or said has resulted in unresolved hurt/resentment in his/her life.*** (It would be wise to check in with your small group to see if they believe your relationship with your spouse is safe enough to have this kind of conversation.)

(Continued on Next Page...)

Do the same thing with your children—individually and age appropriately. (I ask my preschoolers how I am doing in my job as Mommy and if there are things they don't like about me or what I'm doing. I ask my eight year old if I have hurt her feelings in any way or if she is angry with me about anything.)

Broaden your focus on your failures to include significant family members, friends, and co-workers. Ask them about any outstanding debts you owe.

Respond to what you hear with gratitude ("Thanks for being honest.") ***and validation*** ("So you felt very disrespected when I questioned you in front of our friends.").

Apologize for the hurt you have caused and express how you will make amends. (For example, in the situation with my daughter's embarrassment at what I shared with Mrs. Becky, I apologized to Rachel when she shared her hurt and I also apologized to her in front of Mrs. Becky later on, owning that I hurt and embarrassed her by what I shared.)

Talk to your small group members about your failures. Share with them how you plan to make amends in each situation.

Talk to God about your plans. Ask Him to show you how best to make amends in each situation. Write down anything He says to you, and then follow through.

I know it is a challenging assignment, but I also feel confident that God is growing you up in Him. Thanks for being willing to walk with Him through your failures.

Next Assignment: Principle Six, Assignment Two, page 121

Assignment Three -
The Past Meets the Present: Lord, Heal My Wounds

Have I told you how very encouraged I am by your hard work and diligence to do these challenging assignments? I know it is not easy, but I am so excited about what God is doing in your life and heart as a result of these intensive times with Him. Today we'll take one last look at Principle Five. Here it is again.

We explore the wounds from our pasts, acknowledge our sinful choices in response to those hurts, and allow God to transform and heal our hearts.

So far in our journey as we've walked through the third level of assignments in each of the principles, we've recorded significant events of our pasts, uncovered our real beliefs about God, explored what "Life" and "Death" are for us, and allowed the Holy Spirit to expose idols in our hearts. Today we are going to be looking at our timelines again, turning our attention to a very difficult subject—our woundings.

Before we begin, though, I need to emphasize two things. First, we look at our wounds because unhealed wounds cripple us and thwart our progress on the journey. We are not dredging up the past just to cause you more pain. We are looking at your wounds in order to see if they are keeping you from running well in this journey we call life. If in the process of this assignment you become so overwhelmed with fear, despair, or shame that you are unable to function, we want you to seek professional help before continuing with the assignment. Your safety is our highest priority, and we recognize that some wounds are so deep and so painful that it is best to deal with them in the context of a counseling relationship.

Second, I want you to know the truth about yourself. **You are not the sum total of your wounds. Your wounds do not define you, nor do they change the way God feels about you.** Let me say that again. **<u>You are more than your woundings</u>.**

Why am I making such a big deal about this anyway? Well, sometimes when we have been wounded as children we get stuck in our growth and development emotionally and spiritually. Our woundedness has become familiar—"normal" to us. It is so familiar that it feels almost unsafe to experience life in other ways. And false beliefs have grown up in our hearts as well—beliefs that tell us that we are victims, people without choices and without hope. As a victim, we cannot see how our own choices have prevented the healing Christ so desperately wants to bring to our hearts and lives, and we actually begin to feel entitled to our pain and anger and loss. We believe the lie that we can never change, that our wounds have defined who we are and who we always will be.

I say this with great compassion but also with great conviction: in Christ, there are no victims. You may have been *victimized* by others during your life, but you are not defined by what was done to you and what you have suffered. You are defined by your relationship with Christ. He took the role of victim for you on the cross so that you could see yourself as He sees you—a spotless bride.

I do grieve with you over all the hurts and wounds you've experienced. It matters to me and to those of us on the journey with you that you were hurt. Most of all, it matters to God.

Tell me, what do you think I mean when I talk about a wound?

I define a **wound** as *any damage to your soul caused by a hurtful experience or a series of hurtful experiences over time.*

Obviously, if you were sexually abused as a child or adolescent, your soul has been wounded. As a result, instead of seeing yourself as you really are, you may have internalized the idea that you are only loved when you are sexual or maybe you now live with a nagging sense of defectiveness and badness that colors your world. But it's not just sexual abuse that damages us. If you lived with a father who never hurt you physically but also never affirmed you in any way, your soul has been wounded as well. You may see it in your inability to rest, your constant drive to succeed, or your lack of motivation to do anything. Your soul has recorded the wrong message: "If I was a better person, then my dad would notice me," or perhaps for you it is, "I'll never be able to please him, so why even try?" Both kinds of wounds—a traumatic event or a prolonged lack of acceptance and love—are serious. Without the Physician's care, these wounds will eventually infect our lives and incapacitate us emotionally and spiritually.

Sometimes, we don't even recognize that what happened to us was damaging or abusive. For us it was normal. So, before we begin looking at our timelines, let me give you some examples of different kinds of abuse.

Verbal/Emotional Abuse

- Name calling and belittling ("You are so stupid!" or "Can't you do anything right?")
- Using profanity/cursing a person ("You little b-----!")
- Threatening/terrorizing ("You're going to be really sorry you did that when I'm through with you!")
- Threatening abandonment/punishing by abandonment ("If you don't hurry up, I'm going to leave you here by yourself.")
- Disowning ("My child would never act the way you've been acting!")
- Invalidating ("You're too sensitive. That shouldn't have upset you.")
- Shaming ("You are a bad child! You should be ashamed of yourself!")
- Ignoring ("Would you be quiet and leave me alone? Can't you see I'm busy!")
- Embarrassing ("You won't believe the crazy thing he/she did today…")
- Deceiving ("Sure, I'll take you shopping this weekend…" but never following through)
- Depending on a child to meet emotional needs a spouse should meet (emotional incest)

Physical Abuse

- Spanking that leaves marks or bruises
- Slapping a child in the face
- Burning, punching, kicking, pinching, biting, shaking a child
- Restraining a child with ropes/locking a child in a room or closet
- Submerging a child's head in water
- Forcing a child to eat/drink non-food items
- Pulling hair
- Starving a child
- Neglecting proper hygiene of the child (not changing diapers, not bathing, etc.)
- Giving a child alcoholic beverages, drugs, or other dangerous substances
- Leaving a child alone for long periods of time
- Refraining from touching/holding a child—no appropriate physical contact

Sexual Abuse

- Exposing a child to pornography or sexually explicit materials
- Using inappropriate sexual language in a child's presence
- Teasing a child about his/her developing body
- Disrespecting the privacy of a child when he/she is undressing or using the restroom
- Touching a child inappropriately
- Forcing a child to touch another person sexually
- Oral sex, vaginal intercourse, anal sex

Spiritual Abuse

- Telling lies about God ("God's going to send you to hell for that!")
- Using Scriptures to coerce and manipulate ("The Bible says your body is not your own…")
- Hypocrisy—saying one thing and living another
- Legalism—performance-driven life that is rules oriented rather than relationship oriented

And one more thing; if the reality of your life is that you were wounded and those wounds are impacting your life today, I want you to know that there is hope for healing. Yes, you have learned to cope with the pain of your wounds in various ways. Yes, your wounds have impacted and influenced the ways you relate to God and others today. And yes, your wounds can be healed—if you allow the Faithful One full access to your heart.

Are you ready?

Please get out your timeline one more time.

Read through your timeline, particularly focusing on the first two sections—Birth to 18 years old

On your timeline, circle the experiences that you feel wounded your soul significantly. *(Be sure to circle any experiences involving sexual abuse, physical abuse, emotional abuse, spiritual abuse, neglect, abandonment, and trauma.)*

Then answer the following questions in your journal.

- As you think about these experiences, what are you feeling?
- Is there any experience on your timeline you have never shared with anyone? (If so, list it in your journal.)
- Which of these experiences is still impacting you emotionally—you feel great pain, anger, sorrow, fear, guilt, or shame when you remember it?
- How are these wounds impacting you relationally? *(Do you find it hard to be intimate with others? Are you shut down emotionally? Do you struggle to empathize with others? Do you rage? Do you feel needy all of the time?)*
- How are your wounds impacting you spiritually? *(Are you having difficulty trusting God? Can you connect with Him when you are alone? How do you see God?)*
- Were you abused in any way as a child? Explain your answer.

Now I want you to choose a hurtful experience or situation from your childhood or adolescence. (It doesn't have to be a one-time event. It could be an on-going situation like feeling different than others or the disapproval of your father.) ***As you think about it, answer these questions.***

- What did I tell myself during this experience?
- What did I believe about myself?
- What did I tell myself about the other person/people involved?
- Where was God during this experience?
- What did I feel during this experience/situation?
- What did I lose as a result of this experience?
- What fears developed as a result of this event?
- Did I keep this experience and my feelings about it a secret or did I tell someone about it? Explain why.
- How is this event/situation still impacting me today?

When you have finished answering the questions, invite the Father to come and look at your wounds with you. Ask Him to heal your hurts and to free you from their powerful impact on your life. Spend some time listening to Him and enjoying His presence. Be sure to write down anything He says to your heart during this time.

(Continued on Next Page...)

Sometime this week I would like for you to share your hurtful experience and what God showed you about it with someone you trust. You may share with a counselor, a safe friend, or your L.I.F.E. group. I want this very difficult assignment of looking at your wounds to be part of God's gentle healing process in your life and I also want to nudge you forward into the Light so that your wounds can be seen by those who can help.

Finally, if there is anything on your timeline that you have never shared with anyone, I would like for you to seriously consider talking about it with a counselor or with your small group. Secrets will eat you from the inside out, and I long for you to be free. I do want you to know that I trust God's timing for the healing of all of your wounds. If you don't feel comfortable sharing with anyone right now, that's okay. If you are at a place where you feel safe to share with others, however, I encourage you to do so.

I am grateful for your courage. You are greatly loved and accepted.

Next Assignment: Principle Six, Assignment Three, page 127

PRINCIPLE SIX

In fellowship with other believers, we develop intimate relationships where we celebrate God's transforming work in us and continue to address areas of immaturity and weakness.

I couldn't have made it without the group. So often we enable our spouses without even knowing it. In my life I enabled my wife's addiction by not dealing with it when I first discovered the problem and by failing to set appropriate boundaries in our relationship. The beauty of the group for me was that they helped me begin focusing on me instead of trying to fix my wife. –Norm

---

When I started this journey over fifteen years ago, I had few friends who really knew all about me. I wanted people to think I had it all together and that I didn't need help. I felt strong and capable if I could manage life alone. Although I could share with others the parts of my life that were "working" and my "happy" feelings, I did not feel it was important to let anyone know about my problems or my feelings of sadness or loneliness. I saw my role in relationships as someone who helped others or was good company. The rest was private!

Recently, I spent an evening with a new acquaintance, and I was moved by her compliment. As she was leaving she said, "Debbie, you are one of the most authentic people I have ever met." I like to think that what I am feeling, thinking, and believing on the inside is what I look like, sound like, and behave like on the outside. Although being authentic in character is a difficult task (and I am not accomplished at it much of the time), it is a challenge I will continue to pursue.

Of course, the change in my life has only been possible because of the intimate relationships I've developed with other women, who like me, are choosing to change. All of my relationships are richer today because of what I have learned in my safe community of people choosing to examine their lives and seek Godly change. I am a better wife, mom, daughter, sister, friend, and colleague. I am so grateful that I allowed myself to be known by safe people who could help me grow. I am so thankful that I did not stay in isolation. I know the dramatic changes in my life are the result of God's healing and transforming power released in these relationships.—Deb

Tell me, what does "intimate relationship" mean to you?

When we talk about **intimate relationships** in this guide, we are speaking about *authentic relationships in which people are truly known—their thoughts, feelings, desires, fears, beliefs, and dreams are shared with others.* Intimate relationships are always reciprocal. There is the dynamic of both knowing and being known. Intimate relationships are all about emotional and spiritual connectedness.

We've talked about our need for intimacy—authentic relationship. God created us as relational beings. He meant for us to connect with each other and with Him. Unfortunately we learn very early in life that exposing who we really are in relationships often results in rejection and pain. And so we start building walls of protection around our hearts.

Let me pause here for a moment and clarify something. If you were abused as a child—emotionally, physically, or sexually—then the walls you put up in your heart actually helped you to survive. Walls aren't all bad, you know. Appropriate walls or boundaries are necessary for an emotionally and spiritually healthy life. The problem comes when we continue to believe as adults that we must still protect ourselves, and we end up keeping out the good as well as the bad. We get stuck in child-like thinking, and we end up spiritually and emotionally stunted, unable to grow up in our souls. Also, when we put up walls as a result of childhood wounds, we not only separate and protect ourselves from people, we often separate ourselves from God as well.

And that's a problem. ***Why? What do you think?***

God is the only person in your life who will always be Faithful and True. He is the only one with whom you never need to guard your heart, feelings, and emotions. With Him you can be yourself and never fear rejection or abandonment. He loves you unconditionally, all of the time, no matter what you do. Not only that, He created you for Himself. He made you in order to be able to relate to you. He desires you and hungers for your love and devotion. And, that's not all. Not only does He love you and desire relationship with you, He has a vision and a plan for your life. He says in His Word that it's a good plan—a plan to give you a future and a hope (Jeremiah 29:11). And all of the resources of the world are at His disposal to make it happen.

But because of the walls in our hearts, we're unable to experience God in these ways. We don't trust Him. We've interpreted the events of our lives through our own brokenness and with the help of the enemy, and we have come to believe that God is not good and that He is preventing us from experiencing the life we want.

So we don't trust God, and we don't trust people. ***Where does that leave us?***

Alone.

When we feel alone, we also feel rejected and insignificant. And so the pursuit of love and significance begins—bringing us right back to where we are now.

Anyone want to break the cycle?

The only way we can find the life God has intended for us all along is to become connected with Him and other safe people in intimate relationships. Let me say that again: intimate relationships are necessary for our growth and our healing. We will never be who God made us to be apart from authentic relationships with Him and others.

Hopefully by this point on the journey you are beginning to experience a growing intimacy with God and have begun letting others see the real you in your small group. One of the main purposes of your L.I.F.E. group is to give you a safe place to be authentic and to experience true intimacy with those who share similar stories and struggles.

As you continue to grow, our desire and hope for you is that you will begin relating authentically with other believers outside of your small group and will be able to model for them what a genuinely intimate friendship looks like. I know that sounds scary, but don't worry. As you mature you will begin to see more clearly who is safe to invest yourself in and who is best left alone. You will learn how to share bits and pieces of yourself and to judge where another person is on their own journey by their reaction to you. And eventually, you will become a crusader for true intimacy—because once you have tasted real relationship, you will never want to go back to the way life used to be. You'll be living in the reality that God has more for you than you ever thought possible.

But I'm getting ahead of myself. Principle Six says: ***In fellowship with other believers, we develop intimate relationships where we celebrate God's transforming work in us and continue to address areas of immaturity and weakness.*** The three primary action words in this principle are **develop, celebrate**, and **continue**.

We use the word **develop** because intimate relationships don't happen overnight. Building an authentic friendship takes time and intentionality. The second key word **celebrate** communicates the genuine joy that flows from connected hearts as we watch each other grow and change. **Continue** reminds us that the journey is not an event but a process.

So, intimate relationships are growing, developing friendships in which others rejoice in what God is doing in us and help us continue to grow in Him. I love the way Larry Crabb defines a true spiritual friend in his book, *The Safest Place on Earth.* He says that a true friend:

- Enters my world.
- Is intrigued with what God is doing in my life.
- Asks me questions.
- Honors my place on the journey.
- And does all of this with no agenda to "help" or "fix."[vii]

Based on this definition, are you a true spiritual friend? Why or why not?

Do you currently have any true spiritual friends? List their names here.

I hope you have at least a couple of names on your list. We all need true friends and authentic relationships with them to do this journey well. I have one other stretching-growing thing to talk about before we close for the day.

First, tell me, what kind of person do you like to have as a friend? Describe his/her qualities.

Do you see the friend you just described as mostly like you or very different from you? Why?

Sometimes we avoid certain people because they intimidate us or possess qualities we wish we had. And when we are stuck in fear or envy, it is impossible for us to experience true intimacy. In my own life I tended to avoid women who were stylishly dressed and well put together physically. Their beauty and confidence seemed to highlight my own inadequacies, so I made myself comfortable with women like me—motherly, no-nonsense, a little on the frumpy side. Together we pretended that we were happy the way we were while secretly each of us longed to be one of the "pretty people."

Looking back now I see how much I cheated myself of valuable relationships with women who could have taught me much about life and healthy boundaries. My fears and the envy I was struggling with prevented me from experiencing any kind of relationship—much less an intimate one—with women I perceived as different from me.

During my early days in recovery one of my counselors challenged me about the lack of true friends in my life and the type of friends I had. She pointed out that I always chose friends that didn't challenge me or make me feel uncomfortable. And because of my choices, I wasn't growing in relationships. Then she gave me a homework assignment: pursue a friendship with a woman who intimidated me. I have to admit I gave her the evil eye for a few seconds. She was definitely pushing me out of my comfort zone!

But you know what? She was right. In the years since my counselor challenged me, I have had the pleasure to invest myself in friendships with dozens of classy women. I've gained so much from those relationships that I wonder how I ever lived without them.

How about you? Are there certain kinds of people you avoid? People God might want to use in your life to stretch and grow you? (Explain your answer.)

Take the challenge. Invest in safe people that are different from you. You may be surprised to find that they are the ones God will most use in your life to help you grow. Homework time!

Assignment One - Intimate Relationships: The Key to Lasting Change

At the top of a new page in your journal write the heading, "*Intimate Relationships I Desire in My Life*." You will be writing about three kinds of relationships—an intimate relationship with your spouse/children, intimate relationships with friends, and an intimate relationship with God.

Start with your spouse. In your journal, write about what you think an intimate relationship with your spouse would look like. Include ways your spouse would relate to you and ways you would relate to your spouse.

Now do the same thing for your children (if you have any), your friends, and God.

When you are finished you should have at least three lists of qualities of intimate relationships you desire in your life.

With a highlighter, go through what you've written and highlight responsibilities that would be yours in each of those relationships. (Don't highlight any characteristics that are dependent on the choices of others.)

Now look at all the qualities you have highlighted. Are you currently relating in these ways to your spouse, your children, your friends, and God? ***In your journal write about the difference between how you desire to relate and how you relate to God and others right now.***

Then spend some time talking with God about how you would like your relationship with Him to be. Express your desires to Him. Show Him your heart, and don't forget to write down anything He says to you.

Finally, in your small group this week, share what you think an intimate relationship looks like with true spiritual friends. Tell fellow group members how you desire to relate to others, and ask them to hold you accountable for growth in your relationships.

Next Assignment: Principle Seven, page 133

Assignment Two - Boundaries: The Protector of Relationships

Welcome back to Principle Six. Today we'll be talking about how to protect our valuable relationships. Let's look at the principle again.

In fellowship with other believers, we develop intimate relationships where we celebrate God's transforming work in us and continue to address areas of immaturity and weakness.

You've done a lot of hard work building and developing intimate relationships with other believers as we've worked through these principles together. Hopefully you are beginning to experience authentic friendships with members of your small group, with your spouse, with family members, and with other believers God has brought into your life.

Because intimate relationships are so vital to our healing and growth, it is very important for us to learn how to safeguard them from unhealthy and destructive relational dynamics. We do this by setting appropriate boundaries in all of our relationships.

Let's review for a moment. ***What is a boundary?***

Good job! A boundary is a property line—a way we define where we, and our responsibilities, begin and end. Boundary lines make good neighbors. When two people agree on where their yard ends, there is no conflict over who is going to mow what or who is responsible for removing the dead tree that has fallen. Each person has his own yard to care for.

When I first began seeing a counselor five years ago, I had no idea what a boundary was in terms of personal relationships. I understood the importance of boundaries in the physical world but had never carried the same principles into my emotional life. Consequently, Troy and I were terrible neighbors. He would come into my yard and dump his trash. I believed it was my job to take care of his stuff as well as my own yard, so my life became consumed with Troy. Then, on the rare occasions that I finished cleaning up the stuff he had dumped on my side of the fence, I would go into his yard and try to rearrange things the way I wanted them. Neither of us respected each other, and both of us struggled with resentment because of it.

As my counselor described boundaries to me, she drew a picture of a little house with a fenced-in yard on one side of a bridge. On the other side of the bridge she drew another house with a fenced-in yard. She told me that when two people had healthy boundaries, they would relate to each other by crossing the bridge and knocking on the gate. They would not barge in uninvited or throw stuff over the fence without permission. Instead, they would honor the other person in the relationship by taking care of their own yard and asking to enter the yard of their friend.

I remember thinking then that I wished someone had told me about boundaries when I was a teenager. That's when all of my caretaking and enabling started because I believed taking care of other peoples' yards was my God-given job. And I had a lot of practice living that way before I ever met Troy.

How about you? Have you been allowing people to dump stuff in your yard and/or taking care of other peoples' yards for them? Describe what that has looked like in your life.

So, as we develop intimate relationships, we want to be careful not to fall back into unhealthy patterns of relating. The fastest way to lose a friend is to climb over her fence and mow down all of her emerging spring bulbs because you think they are weeds coming up in her lawn. Sound crazy? If we're not careful, we will do the same thing emotionally, unaware of the damage we are causing.

Take Sally for instance. She was molested by her stepfather from the age of five until she eloped with her high school sweetheart when she was fifteen. Her first husband was an alcoholic who beat her when he was drunk, and her second husband was a sex addict who abused her sexually and emotionally. Finally realizing that she must be attracting these abusive men in some way, she has sought help and is seeing for the first time how her past has impacted her. Sally has a huge hole in her heart. She is desperate for male affirmation, and part of her current struggle is learning how to let God meet that need in her heart instead of trying to get that need met by men. Sally has carefully placed protective boundaries in her life to prevent herself from being drawn into another romantic relationship. She's investing herself in female relationships at group and really enjoying herself for the first time in her life.

Let's pretend that one of her new friends is you. As you look at Sally's life and over the fence into her yard, you can tell that she's not very handy. There are a lot of things that need repairing around the house, and you think to yourself, "Sally needs a good man in her life—an honest man who will treat her right. She has so much to offer." And so you begin to invite her to join you at church events—events where you know there will be single and available men for her to meet. It isn't long, of course, before a very sweet guy takes notice of Sally and begins to pay a lot of attention to her. Sally is still too new to recovery to resist his kind words and gentlemanly ways. All of her carefully placed boundaries get pushed aside, and she begins to pursue the relationship wholeheartedly. It's not very long before she stops coming to group and stops investing in female relationships altogether.

What happened?

Yep. You crossed over her fence and mowed down her daffodils—even though your intention was only to help.

What would have been the healthy way to honor Sally and your friendship?

I have a couple of ideas. You could get to know Sally more intimately so that you know where her broken places are and how she is addressing them. Or you might ask about the absence of a man in her life right now and how she feels about it. The important thing to do is to allow Sally to tend her own yard and to ask for help if and when she needs it.

I want you to become aware of the way you are pulled in relationships. Do you instinctively want to help others and solve their problems? Do you seem to have a neon sign on your head that flashes "I will help you" and attracts all kinds of needy people? Or maybe you allow others to use you in relationships and you always find yourself putting your own needs and desires last. Perhaps you are a needy person who feels driven to find stronger more capable others to take care of you and make your decisions for you.

Once you identify your broken places and how you tend to relate to others because of them, it's time to place some well-considered boundaries in your life. For example, if you tend to be a "helper/fixer," you can set a boundary for yourself of refraining from giving advice in your relationships with others. Instead, focus on knowing and being known. "I feel… about… because…" statements are a great way to respond when you want to give advice.[viii]

Friend: "Guys, I don't know what to do! I'm so confused. Part of me wants to ask Ann for a separation while part of me wants her to stay for the sake of the children."

You: "I feel deeply burdened for you because I know what a tough decision you are having to make. And I feel angry at Ann because her behaviors have put you in this difficult situation."

Remember, when we are hurting, we usually don't need advice. What we want to know is that we are not alone—that others understand us.

If you tend to attract every needy person in the world, you can place a boundary in your life of always letting your first response to any requests for help be: "Thanks so much for asking. Let me think about it, and I'll get back to you."

If you are always finding yourself in angry, abusive relationships, you can set a boundary in your life of distancing yourself from those friendships and allowing angry people to experience the consequences of their actions.

If you are a needy person who gravitates toward caretakers, you can put a boundary in your life of not asking for advice. Instead, invest yourself in your relationship with God and learn to give to others—without any strings attached.

The Bible, and especially Proverbs, is full of boundaries that protect relationships. Listen to what the Bible has to say about some of the things we've talked about today.

- ***A fool finds no pleasure in understanding but delights in airing his own opinions.*** (Proverbs 18:2 NIV)
- ***For each one should carry his own load.*** (Galatians 6:5 NIV)
- ***A hot-tempered man must pay the penalty; if you rescue him, you will have to do it again.*** (Proverbs 19:19 NIV)
- ***Let your foot rarely be in your neighbor's house, lest he become weary of you and hate you.*** (Proverbs 25:17 NASB)

Remember, healthy relationships are characterized by boundaries that result in:

- Mutual love and respect
- Interdependence—both people give and receive in the relationship
- Balance—both people invest appropriate time in the relationship but also pursue intimate relationships with others
- Vision—both people see internal qualities rather than external appearances
- Trust—both people feel safe to be themselves
- Growth—both people are focused on God and His work in their hearts
- Authenticity—both people relate to each other with an equal measure of grace and truth

Intimate relationships with others are very valuable. They teach us how to be real, and they help us see how God relates to us. There is one other relationship I want to focus on before we get to the homework, and it is our relationship with our spouse.

Appropriate boundaries are vital to our having an intimate relationship with our mate. Without healthy limits, we will end up dependent on each other and resentful when our spouse is unable to meet our needs.

What do you think is the first step in placing appropriate boundaries in your relationship with your spouse?

I believe healthy limits start with an awareness of what is your spouse's stuff and what is yours. If you wrongly define responsibilities, your relationship will never be safe or intimate. Whenever we are in our spouse's yard trying to "help" him/her, what we are really doing is trying to control life and manage our own levels of pain and discomfort. And when we are controlling, we are not relating authentically.

So, with our spouses, we must begin to mark out the boundary line that says, "This is your property and your responsibility, and this is my yard over here." And we must begin to allow our spouse the opportunity to take ownership of his/her yard.

I know. I can already hear you.

But Melissa, his yard impacts me! He's driving the property value down in the whole neighborhood by the way he neglects his place! He's not some stranger I can turn into the homeowner's association. He's my husband. How am I supposed to live in relationship with him when his yard is such a wreck?

It looks to me like you have three choices.

You could choose to move out of the neighborhood so that you don't have to see your spouse's yard all of the time. Of course, his/her yard won't go away. You'll have to see it when you bring the kids over on the weekends, and you'll probably hear about it from your mutual friends. Option number one may look attractive initially, but it won't solve all of your problems. Recognize that if you make this choice, you will still feel pain and you will still need to learn how to stay out of your spouse's yard.

You could choose to continue the very tiring work of going over to your spouse's place to do the yard work for him/her. At least things will look okay on the outside and you can derive some sense of value from your ability to help. Option number two allows you to keep up the pretense of Life, although it is a choice that results in you being more and more alone.

Or you could choose to admit the truth of the situation to your spouse, acknowledge how his/her behavior is impacting you, and remind your spouse that you have been committed to the relationship from the very beginning. Then you could apologize for the ways you have tried to control and manage your spouse's yard and tell your mate that you realize your behavior has damaged the relationship as much as his/hers has. You might confess that your focus on your spouse's yard has resulted in your own yard becoming a mess. And then you would set the boundary. For a spouse who was still acting out sexually, it might sound something like this:

I want to remain in relationship with you, but the way you are living your life is causing me much pain. I recognize that I am powerless over your choices, and I also know that it is time to guard my heart and take care of my own life. Therefore, I am making a choice to let you be responsible for your choices and to bear the full weight of the consequences that result from them. While you are behaving in destructive ways that hurt me and our marriage, I want you to know that my gate will be closed. You will not be welcome to see my heart or participate in what God is doing in my life. For now I am willing to wait to see if you will come to a place of brokenness and surrender. If and when you reach that place, you are welcome to knock on my gate.

Of course, the boundary would be different for a spouse who was pursuing transformation and healing. You'll get to think about your choices for your situation during the homework today.

Let's do some work on boundaries.

This will be a two-part assignment that will take several hours to do. So don't get discouraged if you are unable to complete it in one day.

In your journal write the heading Boundaries in my Friendships. ***Then complete the following sentences:***

- In my relationships with others I struggle to…
- When I have a conflict in a relationship with someone other than my spouse, the conflict most often is about…
- My friends would characterize me as…
- My greatest strength in relationships is…
- My greatest weakness in relationships is…
- When I see a need in a friend's life I usually…
- When someone needs me or asks me for help I feel…
- When a friend is angry with me I usually…
- When I have a friend who seems more adequate and more significant than me, I tend to….

Now read through what you have written. What broken places in your own heart are influencing the way you relate to others? What boundaries could you put in place in your life to protect your current relationships and promote their growth? (Be as specific and concrete as you can.)

(Continued on Next Page…)

When you are finished with this part of your assignment, call at least two of your friends and share what you feel are weaknesses in the ways you relate to them. Ask them to give you their perspective, and then talk with them about the boundaries you have set for yourself.

The second part of your assignment relates to boundaries in your relationship with your spouse. In your journal write the heading Boundaries in my Marriage Relationship***. Now answer the following questions in your journal.***

- My biggest struggle with boundaries in my marriage is…
- When my spouse does something that hurts or offends me I usually…
- When I hurt or offend my spouse I usually respond by…
- I would say that my spouse and I are good neighbors to each other (rarely, sometimes, most of the time) because…
- My greatest strength in my relationship with my spouse is…
- My greatest weakness in my relationship with my spouse is…
- When I am afraid in my marriage I tend to…

Now make a list of all of the issues/situations that are sources of conflict or resentment in your marriage. In your journal, make three columns with these headings:

My Responsibilities	Spouse's Responsibilities	Shared Responsibilities

Place each of the issues or situations under one of the columns. If you feel that something is a shared responsibility, briefly explain why.

When you are finished, read through your lists and answer these questions:

- In what ways am I trying to take care of my spouse's yard?
- How am I handling what is in my own yard?
- What boundaries do I need to set in order to allow my spouse to take ownership of his/her yard? *(Be as specific and concrete as possible.)*
- What boundaries do I need to set in order to protect my own heart? *(Use the format "If my spouse chooses to…I will feel…and my choice will be…")*

Your final assignment is to draw a picture that depicts the work you have done here. Draw one house with a fenced yard for your spouse and one for you. In the two yards, draw symbols that represent issues that are each of your responsibilities. Then by the fence in your yard, list the boundaries you have set to protect your marriage relationship and to protect your heart when your spouse makes hurtful choices.

Share your drawing with your small group this week. If it is appropriate and possible, set aside a time to share your drawing with your spouse as well.

Next Assignment: Principle Seven, Assignment Two, page 136

Assignment Three - The Past Meets the Present: Overcoming Obstacles to Intimacy

Today we'll take our third look at Principle Six. Let's review it one last time.

In fellowship with other believers, we develop intimate relationships where we celebrate God's transforming work in us and continue to address areas of immaturity and weakness.

So far as we've studied this principle we've talked about building authentic relationships with others and protecting our relationships with appropriate boundaries. In our time together on this third assignment, I want to talk with you about some of the obstacles to intimacy we may encounter on the journey.

Let me begin by asking you what you think. ***What kinds of obstacles to intimacy do you think you might face as you walk in recovery?***

There are actually two different kinds of obstacles we may encounter—obstacles from within our own hearts and obstacles outside of us. It is probably easier to see the outside obstacles we encounter—an unrepentant spouse, hurtful or abusive relationships, etc.—than to admit the roadblocks in our own hearts, but both kinds of obstacles can prevent us from experiencing intimacy and Life the way God intended.

So let's talk about these obstacles. We'll focus on the obstacles we may encounter from within—since we're learning to look at our stuff first. They are:

1. Our desires
2. Temptation
3. Unhealed father wounds
4. Unbelief
5. Wrong goals

We talked about our **desires** in Principle Four. We learned that our desires are not evil, that God created us with desires. Author and psychologist Larry Crabb talks about how every desire we have is ultimately a desire for God when we trace it back to its source.[ix] The problem comes when we try to satisfy our desires apart from Him. Very quickly our desires turn into demands. We come to believe that we need what we want and that God and others are responsible to help us get it. When God and others fail to help us get what we now think we need, these unmet expectations result in great disappointment. Ultimately we punish those we are in relationship with for not giving us what we "need." At this point, our hearts have been captured, and we are now serving creation instead of the Creator—looking for what we desire in places where we can never be satisfied.[x]

How can we keep our desires from blocking intimacy with God and others?

That's right. We share our desires—both the good and the bad—with other believers, trace those desires back to a longing for God, and let our friends keep us accountable for holding our desires with open hands.

Another obstacle we will encounter on the journey is **temptation.** Temptation is inextricably linked to our desires but has the added twist of being aided and abetted by the enemy of our souls. In terms of our pursuit of intimacy, Satan most often uses three of our biggest desires to hi-jack us on the road to authentic relationships—our desire for acceptance, our desire for significance, and our desire to escape pain.

How do you think he uses these desires to tempt us?

Real intimacy is dependent on a commitment to authentic relationship in which we know others and are fully known by them. Satan's temptations come in the form of things that masquerade as intimacy or keep us from feeling pain. Instead of turning to God when we are overwhelmed, we may eat chocolate or go shopping or zone out in front of the TV. Sometimes we become slaves to work or ministry because it gives us a false sense of significance. Or we might become dependent on another human being to satisfy our desire for love and acceptance. All of these behaviors prevent us from experiencing authentic relationship with God and others. And our enemy knows how easy it is for us to live for ourselves instead of honoring our relationship with God. The truth is that we are tempted because our hearts are divided. Part of us is devoted and faithful to our Lord. But another part of us wants to gratify itself—no matter who gets hurt in the process.

The good news is that every temptation is an opportunity to say to God, "I love you and trust Your plans for me." As we become aware of our desires and our places of vulnerability, we can ask others on the journey to watch our backs and keep us accountable. We can also make a daily choice to pledge allegiance to the King of Kings and Lord of Lords from a heart that says, "Your will be done." Finally, we can put boundaries in our life to help us avoid the environments and circumstances that trigger desires we tend to meet apart from Christ.

A third obstacle to intimacy, especially in our relationship with God, is **unhealed father wounds.** Whenever we are inadequately fathered or abused in some way by our dads, we tend to project their failures onto our heavenly Father. We believe the same things about Him as we do about them. You've done some challenging work already on your beliefs about God and unhealed wounds in your heart.

What parallels have you found between your past hurts and your beliefs about God?

In order to pursue an intimate relationship with God wholeheartedly, you will have to deal with the wounds in your heart caused by your earthly father. Your group will be able to help you talk about those hurts and beliefs, and you may also need the help of a professional counselor to sort through what is true about your dad that is not true about God.

Closely connected to unhealed father wounds is a huge stumbling block for many of us on the journey. This obstacle is **unbelief**. Our enemy takes our wounds and uses them as a tool to prevent us from knowing God and trusting Him. Satan comes to us when we are innocent children and begins feeding us his lies and deception. And since we often have no one to model what really is true about God for us, we believe the lies.

What do you think is the biggest lie Satan wants us to believe about God?

If our enemy can get us to believe that God is not good then we will never experience intimacy. For if we don't believe God is good, we will never trust Him. And if we cannot trust Him, we will find it very difficult to enter into relationship with Him. And if we don't enter into relationship with Him, the enemy has won our soul. Don't be ignorant of Satan's devices. He will use anything he can against you to destroy you. And if he can't take you to hell with him, he will do everything in his power to make you a powerless and ineffective Christian.

So if you are struggling to trust God, what can you do? The interesting thing about faith struggles created by woundings is that I can throw Scriptures at them all day long and never feel any different about God. My head knows all of the right things, but my heart declines to agree. The intellectual knowledge in my mind does not match the experiential knowledge of my heart, and when put to the test, our hearts will almost always overrule our heads. Somehow, we've got to get all of that *knowledge about God* in our minds to become *knowing God* in our hearts.

I have found on my own journey that it is very helpful to continue immersing myself in the truth of God's Word. It is also crucial to connect with other believers so that I can experience intimate and loving relationships with them. But the only way my heart is fully convinced that God is faithful and good and loving and just and present and powerful is if my *heart* ***experiences*** Him in those ways.

It's not necessarily some mystical process of seeing visions or hearing an audible voice—although it can be. God is so infinitely creative. He allows us to experience Him in a myriad of ways. He's always at work in our lives and around us. He is ever present and ever involved. We just don't know how to look for Him.

We'll talk more about experiencing God in Principle Seven, but for now let me just say that if you struggle with unbelief, make a point of asking God to show Himself to you during your times with Him. You'll be amazed at how He answers your prayers.

Finally, a fifth obstacle that sometimes trips us up on the road to intimacy is **wrong goals**. A lot of times when we start the journey after the initial disclosure of our spouse's sexual addiction, we have goals like making our marriage work, being a better wife or husband, "helping" our spouse with his/her recovery, learning what sexual addiction is and how to fix it, keeping all sexually explicit material out of our home, etc. They are understandable goals, but as you grow emotionally and spiritually you will come to understand that goals like these can prevent you from experiencing intimacy with your spouse and with God.

Why? What do you think?

When we cannot accept or envision a bigger goal than getting our spouse "fixed" or "healed" from sexual addiction, we come up against a *huge* obstacle on the journey. We have a goal that we are powerless to achieve. And so two things happen. We become controllers, trying to make our goal become a reality. And we get stuck emotionally, becoming extremely tired. Our emotions are constantly yo-yoing from hopeful (when spouse is doing well) to distraught (when spouse is not doing so well). We get so tired of it all we either detach emotionally or medicate our pain and fatigue in sinful ways.

If goals that are dependent on others are obstacles on the journey, what kind of goals do we need to be setting?

You got it! Goals about us. Goals about our own spiritual and emotional growth and development. Goals that reflect God's agenda for us and not our own. The truth is that "goals" that depend on the choices of others are not goals at all; they are desires. And desires are to be expressed to God and others truthfully while being held with open hands.

I can guess what you're thinking. *Okay, Mel. I hear what you are saying. There are lots of things in my own heart that can block an intimate relationship with God and others. But if I can't get what I want—a faithful spouse who loves me and is devoted to God and family—is there really any hope for this Life you keep talking about?*

And that trust thing. How can I learn to trust God when it seems He's been just as unfaithful as my spouse?

Wow! Two big questions. I think what you are asking me is: Can I have Life if my deepest desires are not satisfied, and can I trust God when Life is painful?

I'm reminded of a story when I think about those questions. Once upon a time there was a father and mother who had three children. One of them was a boy named Lazarus, and he had two sisters named Mary and Martha. Time passed and the father and mother died. The siblings lived together in the same village, and they stayed closely connected. And they had a very good friend who stayed at their house from time to time when he was traveling. The four were very close. This friend's name was Jesus.

Then Lazarus became ill. The sisters sent for their friend. They believed He was from God, the promised Messiah, and that He could heal any sickness. They had great faith in His love for them and His ability to heal their brother. But Jesus did not come—not until it was too late and Lazarus had died.

Martha, the elder sister, met Jesus outside the village. "Lord, if you had been here, my brother would not have died! Even now I know that whatever You ask of God, God will give You." Jesus assured her that her brother would rise again. "I am the resurrection and the life; he who believes in Me shall live even if He dies, and everyone who lives and believes in Me shall never die. Do you believe this?" He asked Martha. "Yes, Lord," she replied. "I have believed that you are the Christ, the Son of God, even He who comes into the world." But Martha thought Jesus was talking about the afterlife—not her present. She left Him and went to tell her sister that Jesus had come.

Mary ran to her friend Jesus, wailing, "Lord if You had been here, my brother would not have died!" And Jesus, deeply moved in His heart, wept.

There they were, three friends intimately connected who loved and trusted each other completely grieving over the loss of one of their own. The pain was intense. The loss was a reality. The sisters grieved two losses—the loss of their brother and the loss of a dream. If only Jesus had come in time. They never doubted Jesus' love for them nor His power to heal their brother. What they were grappling with was why someone who loved them and was able to help in a time of great need was absent when they needed Him most.

Jesus grieved too. He saw their pain. He knew their deepest desires, but He also understood God's agenda. What the sisters could not see or understand was that God's plan for Lazarus was different from theirs. Mary and Martha wanted Lazarus to be healed before he died. God wanted to show the world that in Christ there is no death.

And having directed them to remove the stone in front of the tomb, Jesus cried out with a loud voice, "Lazarus, come forth!" What was dead, was made alive again. The sisters had regained a brother, and Jesus still had a friend.[xi]

I wonder if you've ever felt like Mary and Martha did that day. Are there any "if onlys" preventing you from giving all of yourself to God?

Are the beliefs in your head stopping short of your heart?

Is your pain blinding you to God's bigger agenda for your life?

Are you defining Life by the absence of pain instead of the person of Christ?

Yes, there are obstacles. And, they can be overcome. We'll stop here and do some homework.

We'll spend some time journaling first. ***Please answer the following questions honestly***.

- Which of the obstacles we discussed today do you see in your own heart?
- Which of your desires does the enemy most often use in your life to tempt you?
- When do you find yourself most vulnerable to temptation?
- Which unhealed father wounds is the enemy using to distort your perception of God?
- How are you promoting the healing of those wounds?
- Which safe people in your life know about your woundings and how they have impacted you? List their names.
- In what ways do you struggle to trust God?
- In what ways do you see God at work in your heart and life?
- What wrong goals have been driving your life?

In your small group this week, talk to your fellow journeyers about the obstacles you see in your heart and how you desire to change.

The next part of your assignment will take a week to do. ***Your task is to intentionally focus on God's presence in your life and what He is doing around you. For the next week, carry around your journal or small notebook and write down every time God speaks to your heart, does something for you, or is obviously at work in the heart of someone you meet.***

Don't forget to list the unexpected blessings He gives you—a front row parking spot at Wal-Mart, a kind note from a friend, a polite stranger who helps you in some way, a sermon that speaks to your heart, a song that touches your soul. The Bible teaches us that every good gift is from Him—just because He loves us and delights to give us pleasure.

Be constantly on the lookout for His presence and His activity during this week, and whenever you see Him do something, talk to Him about how you feel when you know He is with you.

At the end of the week, take your notebook to group and share your experiences with your friends.

Next Assignment: Principle Seven, Assignment Three, page 138

PRINCIPLE SEVEN

As we consistently walk in grace and truth, we carry the message of Christ's healing to other spouses and pursue a vision of God's purpose for our lives.

Unfortunately, not many men married to female sex addicts take the healing journey of recovery. The shame and feelings of inadequacy are so great that often men just suffer in silence. I know women struggle with that too. I'm really grateful that God gave me the desire to seek wholeness and transformation for myself—even though my ex-wife chose not to do the journey. The healing He has brought into my life as a result of my willingness to embrace His truth about me and intimate relationships with safe people is so worth the time and tears I have invested. I still hurt for my kids as I see how all of this has impacted them. But I am hopeful for them too because God is faithful.

I'm married now to a woman who knows me at every level and shares herself with me in the same way. We have a truly intimate relationship—one that would not be possible had I failed to take the journey. This past year I've been able to share my story with others and build deeper friendships with men in my church and community. My hope is that my story will encourage other men who are married to female sex addicts to embrace recovery for themselves. It's exciting to think about what God has in store for me, and it's wonderful to be a part of something bigger He is doing through me. –Norm

---

Our time in Fresno had come to an end. We were moving to Georgia, a place where we had never lived and where I (Melissa) had no friends. My counselor and I were talking about the move and how I felt about it. I expressed my concern that Troy and I had no relationships for accountability there. I told her how much the group at New Creation Ministries had come to mean to me. Then Dawn said to me, "Well, Melissa, is there any reason why you couldn't start your own spouse's group? Perhaps God is initiating a new call on your life."

In the months that followed, my counselor's words kept coming to my mind. The first year in Georgia was very lonely for me. We were starting over, I was pregnant, and I had two other preschoolers to care for. I had no time or energy for relationships, and I longed for my friends at NCM. It was during that year that the Lord began to peel back some of the hidden layers of brokenness in my own life, helping me to see that Troy was not the only one who had deep issues to deal with. And my motivation to have intimate relationships grew.

One day I sat down with an assistant pastor at church and shared about my loneliness and my desire to have some accountability in my life. I told him how much the group at NCM had meant to me and helped me grow. His next sentence was a question, "Melissa, would you be willing to start that kind of group here?"

Six months later, after the Father had done some additional pruning and preparation in my heart, the first meeting of Journey took place. We started with five women plus me and today we have grown to over thirty women who meet regularly every week. And the Lord has so enriched my life with relationships. He's given me a passion to help other spouses walk this journey and to walk it with grace and truth. And all the while He's been growing me up, transforming me from the inside out.— Melissa

Today we come to a very important principle. It's a principle about giving back what God has given you. Hopefully you are beginning to understand that the pain in your life is pain for His purposes. You are walking this path because of good plans He has for you. I know it's the valley of the shadows right now, but on the other side there is a hope and a future. You have been through deep waters and there are deeper ones yet to come. In the process, though, God is completing you, and I promise you, it is worth the journey.

The first way we give back to others is by learning how to develop intimate relationships that are characterized by authenticity, grace, and truth. That means you are being real about who you are, speaking the truth to those you love, and allowing God to offer His grace to others through you. We've talked about intimate relationships already, and we'll talk about them much more as we work through the second and third tiers of assignments for the seven principles. When you allow yourself to be known and make the effort to know God and others, you are living out God's first purpose for your life. And your life encourages those around you.

The second way we give back to others is by beginning to speak the truth about our lives and to acknowledge what God is doing in our hearts. When we tell the truth and we allow people to see God at work in us, we give others hope. They come to believe that if God can heal and grow us in the midst of such difficult circumstances, there must be hope for them as well.

You will discover as you walk this journey that the greatest joy to be found is in helping others to see—both by your life and your words—that there is hope and Life in Christ. I am eager to see you start giving back what the Father has given you. You have so much to offer to this world. Seeing you realize your potential in Christ is one of my greatest passions.

With that in mind, I'll give you your first homework assignment for this principle.

Assignment One - Telling My Story

I know you've already shared your story—at least parts of it with your small group. Today, however, I want you to write your story in your journal. This first account will become a mile marker on your journey—one you can look back at down the road and see how far you've come.

In your journal, write the heading My Story. ***Include the following parts of your story in your writing:***

- Tell how you first discovered your spouse's sexual addiction and how you felt in that moment.
- Talk about how your spouse responded to being exposed.
- Describe how his/her choices impacted you.
- Talk about how your relationship with God was impacted by your discovery.
- Share how you came to join your LIFE group.
- Relate how you felt when you first became a part of the group.
- Describe where you are emotionally right now.
- Tell what you've learned and experienced as a part of the group.
- Describe the current state of your marriage.
- Talk about how your current situation is impacting your relationship with God.
- Share what your hope is for the future.

After you have finished writing your story, take some time to sit and reflect on all that you are feeling. Talk to God about your story. Think about what you are thankful for in your story and express your gratitude to Him. Ask Him to continue to heal the wounded parts of your heart. Reaffirm your hope in His good plans for you.

Then, bring your story to group this week to share with your friends.

Thanks for your hard work. I'm glad you are on the journey.

Next Assignment: Principle One, Assignment Two, page 58

Assignment Two - Telling the Rest of My Story

Congratulations! You've made it the last assignment on the second tier. I'm proud of all your hard work and excited about our assignment today. Let's review Principle Seven before we begin:

As we consistently walk in grace and truth, we carry the message of Christ's healing to other spouses and pursue a vision of God's purpose for our lives.

When we first told our stories, we focused on our how spouse's sexual addiction had impacted us and how God was beginning to use our L.I.F.E. group in our lives. Today the focus of our stories will be different.

Talk to me for a moment.

How are you different today than when you first began attending a L.I.F.E. group?

What is the most impacting thing God has shown you about yourself or Himself so far?

What has the journey come to mean to you?

When we first begin the journey, most of us get involved in recovery so that we can get our marriage fixed and go on with life. By now some of you are pretty sure that life will never be the same again. And some of you are actually grateful for that reality. My prayer is that you will continue to give God permission to reshape you and change you rather than expecting Him to try to glue back together the shattered pieces of your life.

Today we are going to tell our stories again—but from a different perspective. This time I want you to tell the story of how God is transforming you. I can't wait to hear your heart!

In your journal, write the heading The Rest of My Story. ***Include the following parts of your story in your writing:***

- Describe your initial motivation for coming to group and talk about your primary goals at that time.
- Talk about when you first realized that you had stuff you needed to work on and how you came to that point on your journey.
- Share about how the relationships in group have impacted your life.
- Relate how God is changing your beliefs about Him and about yourself.
- Describe the most important things you have learned so far in your time on the journey.
- Tell how the way you relate to God and others has changed as a result of what you are learning.
- Talk about your goals now as you allow God to heal and change you.
- Finally, if you could share one thing with a spouse who was just starting the journey, what would it be?

After you have finished writing, reflect on how you are feeling. Invite God to praise you for the changes you've allowed Him to make in your heart. Enjoy the fact that you are growing. If you feel discouraged, talk to the Father about it. Ask Him His perspective on where you are right now, and allow Him to encourage you with His presence and His truth.

Pray about whom God might want you to encourage this week by sharing your story. Jot down any names He brings to your mind, and set aside a time this week to call, email, or meet with the person God puts on your heart.

If it is possible, take time to share this part of your story with your spouse as well.

Finally, share the rest of your story in small group this week.

Great work! I'm encouraged by what God is doing in your life!

Next Assignment: Principle One, Assignment Three, page 61

Assignment Three - The Present Meets the Past: Surrendering My Agenda and Embracing God's Vision for Me

I can't believe we've already made it to this place in our time together. And you are looking like a different person these days. *How are you feeling as you approach this final assignment?* (Check and explain all that apply.)

- ❑ Grateful because ____
- ❑ Sad because ____
- ❑ Anxious because ____
- ❑ Excited because ____
- ❑ Encouraged because ____
- ❑ Discouraged because ____
- ❑ ______________ because ____

Let's review Principle Seven one last time.

As we consistently walk in grace and truth, we carry the message of Christ's healing to other spouses and pursue a vision of God's purpose for our lives.

Today we are going to be talking about a vision of God's purpose for your life. Embracing God's agenda for your life involves two actions on your part. First, you must lay down your agenda for yourself, and second, you must take up His. The focus of our two-part assignment today will be surrendering your agenda—your plans for your life—to the Faithful One and embracing God's agenda—His vision for your life—instead.

You've grown enough to know that the way you have lived in the past has not always been a reflection of God's agenda for your life. And, hopefully you have come to the place where you trust the Faithful One enough to surrender your goals and plans to Him and are ready to embrace whatever He has for you. Of course, the process of laying down and taking up is a journey, one that often involves growing pains.

One of the most painful things He has called me to do as I have walked this journey is to surrender my agenda and embrace His for me with my whole heart. When I made the decision to follow Christ and received Him as my Lord and Savior as a child, I actually committed myself to God's agenda for me. I just didn't realize at the time what that commitment involved and how bent I was on keeping my agenda for me intact. The number one item on my agenda, of course, was being loved and desired by a man. Coming in a close second was my desire to be a godly Christian who let my light shine for the world. I thought these things were on God's agenda for me as well, so I embraced them passionately and did everything I could to make them happen.

And so, when my world fell apart and the husband I had married to love and desire me actually was loving and desiring every one but me, and my missionary career of being light to a dark world was suddenly over, I became very disoriented. God and I had a lot of talks about where I went wrong and how did I miss His plans and how could this happen.

What I have realized in the ensuing years is that for most of my Christian life I operated under the assumption that if I did what I was supposed to do, then God would give me the desires of my heart. I actually based that belief on a Scripture in Psalm 37:4—"Delight yourself in the Lord, and He will give you the desires of your heart (NIV)." I wanted to be loved by a man who cherished and valued me. It wasn't a bad desire, but it became idolatrous in my life. I wanted my man's love more than I delighted in God's love for me. I wanted to be salt and light—a great desire according to God's Word. But my ministry became idolatrous as well. I served to gain the approval of others instead of from a heart that was fully approved of by God. I loved and served from my emptiness instead of from the fullness of God in me. And so, unknowingly, I kept my own agenda while claiming to be (and believing I was) following God's.

So, God in His mercy, took out His surgeon's knife and lovingly but deliberately cut open my heart. And this is what He said, "Child, you gave me this heart a long time ago, but you've taken it back, and in your own strength you've not cared for it well. This is major surgery. I need to cut out diseased tissue, reconstruct and repair what is damaged, and change your lifestyle in order for you to be whole. Since you are Mine and I love you, as painful as it is, this is the way it must be. It will take you a while to recover, but if you will trust Me and follow My agenda instead of your own, your heart will heal and grow, and you will find what you long for in Me."

It was very painful. The initial time of recovery was intensely uncomfortable and difficult. Adjusting to the tremendous lifestyle change was challenging, and I grieved the things I lost. And yet, today, I can honestly say that I would not trade the pain. The Father has kept His promise and He is daily transforming my heart—healing me, growing me. It is still a daily decision to lay down my agenda and to embrace His. Some days I fail. When I do, I am accountable to others on the journey who love me, correct me, encourage me, and support me as I get back on the path. I tell you this to offer you hope and realistic expectations. Change is possible. You will fail sometimes, and God is faithful.

The first part of your assignment today is the laying down and surrendering of your agenda—your goals and plans for your life. So get out your journal and a box of Kleenex.

First, think about all of your desires, goals, and plans for all the different areas of your life.

In your journal, write the heading "My Agenda," and list all of the desires, goals, dreams, and plans that come to your mind.

Now read through the list. Underline or highlight the five desires or goals that you most want to see realized.

Enter into a time of prayer. Tell the Father how you feel about each of your top five desires/goals. Express your longings, your fears, your feelings, your thoughts about each one. Confess any ways you have allowed your agenda to rule your heart.

On a separate sheet of paper, draw a symbol that represents each of these top five desires/goals. Then lay down your drawings in front of God and surrender your agenda to Him. Give Him permission to fulfill His good plans for you. And remind Him that you are growing in your trust, that you want to completely trust Him with every area of your heart and life.

Be sure to write down anything He says to your during this time with Him.

Note: Please stop for the day after completing the first part of Assignment Three, and pick up here tomorrow or later this week.

We've laid down our agenda. Now let's talk about embracing His.

The Bible tells us in Proverbs 29:18 (NASB) that "*where there is no vision, the people are unrestrained.*" You may have heard the verse quoted from the King James Version which says, "Where there is no vision, the people perish." Obviously it is a serious matter when people don't have a vision.

Why? What do you think?

When we don't know what we are living for, when our lives have no meaning or purpose, we throw off all constraint and control and live selfish, indulgent lives. The mindset becomes, "if this is all there is, we might as well enjoy it while we can." And when we live like our greatest purpose in this life is to gratify and satisfy our every desire and to keep ourselves from feeling pain, we become useless—of no good to anyone. Quite often we also cause others a great deal of sorrow.

So having a vision is important. ***But what exactly is a vision? Define it in your own words.***

When we talk about a **vision** in this guide, we are talking about something more than a goal or a plan. We are talking about *an ability to see the big picture—an understanding of God's agenda for your life.*

Think about the people throughout history who have allowed God's vision for them to guide their lives. Abraham's vision was to become the father of many nations. Moses' vision was to lead God's people out of slavery into the Promised Land. Joshua's vision was that he and his house would serve the Lord. Esther's vision was to save her people. Nehemiah's vision was to rebuild the wall of Jerusalem. Solomon's vision was to build the temple of God. Isaiah's vision was to proclaim freedom to the captives. John the Baptist's vision was to prepare the way for the Lord. Jesus' vision was to make a way for us to have Life. The list could go on. Every one of these people laid aside their own plans and goals in order to embrace the will of the Father. Many risked their lives to carry out the vision. Some gave their lives in order to fulfill it.

When we have a vision for our lives, our focus is kept centered on fulfilling what God has called us to do. We live differently. We live carefully, we live wisely, and we live purposefully.

Today we are going to spend some time asking the Father what His vision is for our lives. But I want to give you a few words of instruction before we begin the assignment.

1. God's vision for you is about *you.* It's bigger than your marriage and your family, and it is not dependent upon the choices of those you love. So, don't think about a vision in terms of your marriage or your children. Think about a vision that is God's for you alone.

2. God is the giver of the vision. You are the keeper of the vision. Don't get the two confused. You can't create your own vision and expect God to help you fulfill it. He doesn't work in our lives that way. He gives us His vision for us, and we are responsible to live to make the vision a reality.

3. God's vision for you is bigger than a vocation or a calling. There was a time that I felt God's vision for me was to be a missionary. Being a missionary, though, wasn't my vision; it was my calling and vocation for a time in my life. His vision for me has always been bigger than any career or ministry. His vision for me is to bring good news to those who are brokenhearted and to proclaim freedom for those held prisoner by their own desires and fears. My calling and vocation have changed, but His vision for me has not.

4. God's vision for you is uniquely yours. He created you and equipped you for a vision that only you can fulfill. You are a beautiful thread in the tapestry of His grace. As you think about His vision for you, don't discount the times of deepest hurt and pain and in your life. The pain has had a part in shaping you for His purposes and use.

5. God's vision for you is His signature on your heart. It reminds you daily of His love and His presence. It helps you remember that your life has meaning and significance, that you are important to the Most High God. Once you have understood His big picture and the vision He has for your life, hold onto it with all of your heart. Let it be the passion that sets your life apart and makes a difference in the lives of others.

Are you ready to see what He has for you?

I want you to be aware that this assignment may take you several days of focused prayer and time with the Father. Because you are on His time table and His agenda, He may not show you His vision for your life immediately. But please don't be discouraged. Every moment that you spend with Him seeking His heart and straining to hear from Him is an investment in an eternal relationship—an investment that will have great returns.

So hang in there. The God of all grace and truth will show you His vision for you when He knows you are ready to receive it.

I hear Him calling to you. Do you hear Him? He is saying, "***Call to Me, and I will answer you, and I will tell you great and mighty things, which you do not know***" *(Jeremiah 33:3 NASB).*

In your journal, write the heading God's Vision for Me.

Have your Bible with you, and enter into a time of prayer. Take some time to worship Him and to thank Him for who He is in your life. Ask Him to make His presence known to you. Tell Him you have a request. Ask Him what His vision is for your life, and wait for His reply.

He may bring a Scripture to your mind. He may speak a phrase or a word into your heart.

When you hear from Him, write down what He has told you*. Then ask the Father to confirm that what you have written is His vision for you through His Word and the relationships with other believers He has put in your life.*

You will also know in your spirit that He has spoken into your life. You will probably feel a curious mixture of peace, excitement, and fear—peace because His Spirit within you is at rest, excitement because He has spoken to your heart, and fear because living out the vision is a life-long journey.

When you feel confident that you have heard from God, memorialize His vision for you in some way. *Have a plaque made. Cross-stitch and frame it for your wall. Etch it in stone. Inscribe it over a door in your home. Paint a picture. Write a poem or a song. Do whatever it takes to make this vision the focus of your life.*

Also, share the vision God has given you with those you love—your spouse, your children, your family members, your friends in group. *Ask them all to help you be faithful in keeping the vision God has placed on your life.*

Debbie, Norm, and I are grateful to have been a part of your journey for this little while. May God's grace and truth keep you on the path until you reach the finish line.

Appendix A

L.I.F.E. Group Meeting Format

Facilitating a L.I.F.E. Group meeting is not difficult if you remember that the goal of all L.I.F.E. Groups is authentic relationships that help promote change. As a facilitator the most important aspect of your ministry is being real and open about your own journey. We encourage you to be creative as you lead. Don't feel that you have to stick to this format exclusively. We would like for you to include the different elements of the format in some way during the meeting. However, we want you to have the freedom to adjust the format to fit the needs of your L.I.F.E. Group.

For example, in the group I facilitate, we open with music. Singing together creates an atmosphere of worship and community that helps spouses clear their minds and focus on group. We then go on to pray and open our large group time with introductions and recognition of newcomers.

Also, remember that some of the elements of the meeting format will need to be adjusted based on the size of your group. Since my group has 30 current active members, we omit the group introductions during the large group time and introduce ourselves only in small group time. Your priority as a group facilitator is to make sure there is time for people to relate authentically. Therefore, small group discussion should always be given the most time and priority.

Here is the basic model for a L.I.F.E. Group Meeting:

1. **Opening Introduction and Prayer**

   The group leader introduces herself/himself by first name and describes the name and purpose of the group. The leader then prays or leads the group in saying a prayer together.

   Ex] *"My name is Melissa, and I facilitate this L.I.F.E Group for Spouses. The people in this room are seeking healing and transformation as they deal with their spouses' sexual addiction and their own personal struggles. I'm grateful for your courage to take this painful journey. Let's pray as we begin."*

2. **Group Introductions**

   The group leader invites participants to introduce themselves by first name. Members can also add a statement about where they are on the journey of healing.

   Ex] *"My name is _______, and I'm grieving all of the losses I've experienced because of my spouse's sexual addiction."*

   Ex] *"My name is _______, and I'm working to overcome my struggle with codependence."*

   Ex] *"My name is _______, and I'm new tonight."*

3. Welcome New Members

L.I.F.E. Groups are always open to new members or attendees who are seeking help.

The leader asks if anyone is attending for the first time. After pausing for a show of hands, the leader welcomes them and explains expectations for their first group meeting.

Ex] *"Is anyone here for the first time tonight? We are so glad you have joined us. At your first meeting you aren't expected to share, but we will be honored if you do. There may be opportunities for you to share in this large group session or after we break up into smaller groups. But most importantly, this is a time for you as a newcomer to listen and to start feeling safe. Also, we believe an important practice for everyone on the journey of healing and transformation is to use a mentor or sponsor to help support them during this time. If you would like a temporary mentor/sponsor for the next week(s), please see me after the meeting. Also, if you have any questions about our L.I.F.E. Group and how it functions, I'll be happy to talk to you at the end of the meeting."*

4. Readings

The leader reads the **L.I.F.E. Group Safety Guidelines** if newcomers are present. He/She may also have another group member read a short devotion, the **Seven Principles**, or **How to Get the Most out of L.I.F.E.**

5. Offering

The leader explains the purpose of the offering as she/he passes around a container.

Ex] *"There are no dues or fees for membership in this L.I.F.E. Group, and all are welcome regardless of their ability to make a contribution. However, all L.I.F.E. Groups are self-supporting. We pay for our own materials, rent* (if applicable*), and other expenses, and we contribute to L.I.F.E. Ministries International. We suggest $5 weekly as a contribution to your own healing and to ensure others have access to the help that you've found. Like an offering at a church, you are not required to give, and you're certainly free to give more than the suggested amount."*

6. Business

The leader leads the group in any discussion of old and new business. Old business includes matters such as meeting times and places and ordering of materials. New business includes matters such as special but related events outside of the group or any announcement of matters pertaining to the group's well being.

All decisions are made through the consensus of group members and must be consistent with the policies of L.I.F.E. Ministries. When in doubt, check with the national office.

Ex] *"Is there any old business we need to discuss?"*

"Is there any new business or announcements that affect the group as a whole?"

7. **Discussion of Principle**

The leader or some other group member will have prepared a presentation and/or lead a discussion on the Principle being considered that night. The presentation/discussion should be limited to no more than 20 minutes.

Ex] *"Mary will now lead us in discussing Principle 1, which is: we admit that we cannot control the desires or choices of our spouses, and we acknowledge that our lives have become unmanageable."*

8. **Small Group Discussion**

This is a time of sharing stories, accountability, confession, and building relationships. If you have a Time for Grieving small group, direct newcomers there. In that setting they will be offered a chance to share their story and what has brought them to group. Spouses working through the Seven Principles may divide up into a different small group(s).

Leaders may choose to assign group members to a certain group in order to establish and maintain a more consistent group dynamic. Or they may choose to count off in such a way that small groups are created each week that consist of four or five spouses, including the small group leader.

Note: *A small group should not be larger than seven participants and one group facilitator. When more than seven participants attend, a second small group should be formed.*

Activity during Groups:

Each breakout group should be led by someone with appropriate experience and maturity. The small groups meet for approximately one hour, dividing the time equally among the members.

A. **Time for Grieving Group**
   - Feelings check (how members are feeling physically, emotionally, and spiritually).
   - Invite newcomers to share their story. Group members respond by telling how they identify with the story and how they are feeling as a result.
   - Invite members to share homework assignments with the group.
   - Invite all participants to share prayer requests.
   - Have group members pray for each other.

B. **Seven Principles Group**
   - Feelings check (how members are feeling physically, emotionally, and spiritually).
   - Leader reminds members of the Principle in focus for the meeting.
   - Members share homework assignments for that Principle.
   - As time allows, members share what is currently going on in their lives and any prayer requests they have.
   - Group participants pray for each other.

9. Closing Comments, Reading, and Prayer

Small groups reconvene for a final time together. The group leader thanks all for coming and reminds participants of the next scheduled meeting. He/She also emphasizes confidentiality. The leader may choose to close with another reading and prayer or simply with prayer.

Ex] "*I thank everyone for coming tonight and want to remind you that the next meeting is next Wednesday at 7 p.m. in this room. We have schedules of other area L.I.F.E. meetings as well as phone lists of group members willing to receive calls. If anyone has unfinished individual business, you're encouraged to talk with your mentor/sponsor or small group members this week. Please remember that individual anonymity provides the safety for us to risk being vulnerable to others and exposing our secrets to God's transforming light. Who you saw here and what was said here, let it stay here. Let's close in prayer.*"

Suggested Time Guidelines for Meeting

The timeline for a standard meeting of approximately two hours looks like this:

Welcome, Opening Prayer, and Introductions	5 minutes
Welcome new members	2 minutes
Share devotion/readings	8 minutes
Offering and business discussion	5 minutes
Principle presentation and discussion	20 minutes
(Time to break up into small groups)	5 minutes
Small Groups	65 minutes
(Time to return to large group)	5 minutes
Reconvene and closing	5 minutes
Total Meeting Time	2 hours

Appendix B

Glossary of Terms

Communication is essential to intimate fellowship. Fellowship is vital to L.I.F.E.—living in freedom everyday. Group discussions, feedback, and presentations are the life-blood of support and encouragement. Effective communication and fellowship require that we understand each other—that we speak the same language. Standard terminology is a tool for clear communication, and agreement about definitions allows each L.I.F.E. Group member to communicate easily with others in his/her own group and in the ministry network across the country. This glossary is provided for all L.I.F.E. Group members in order that they may become familiar with the terminology used in L.I.F.E. Group meetings. (The glossary itself may also provide a productive discussion topic for a L.I.F.E. Group meeting.) The definitions are based on Dr. Laaser's understanding gleaned from talking to hundreds of recovering people from a variety of geographic locations. Every group, however, may have local or personal understandings that are important in their setting. What's crucial is that the group discusses variations in meanings so that everyone can be clear about them.

90 Days

The term "Ninety Days" comes from the AA slogan "90 days, 90 meetings," which refers to the first three months of an alcoholic's recovery. Many times it's necessary for a person to go to a meeting every day for the first 90 days in order to remain sober. This commitment is a good one for sex addicts as well. In the beginning of an addict's healing journey or after a relapse, committing to a "90 in 90" is an excellent plan.

Ninety days has also been applied to the period of time a sex addict may choose to be sexually abstinent with self and others, including his/her spouse. This time period allows the addict to "de-tox" from the physiological component of sexual addiction as well as to begin to confront the lie that sex is his/her greatest need.

For spouses, ninety days refers to a commitment to abstain from a particular coping strategy for three months. The purpose of this fast from a particular behavior or substance is to help the spouse realize how much he/she is depending on things other than God for comfort and also to help the spouse begin to understand the powerlessness of addiction. (You'll find more information about the concept of a ninety days abstinence period in Principle Four, Assignment Three.)

Abstinence

This is the state of being non-sexual with self or others. For some addicts, abstinence may also indicate a planned time-out from any romantic relationship.

Accountability Partner

This is any person who agrees to be in your network of people holding you accountable. A common mistake is thinking that you can have only one accountability partner. A person cannot recover or heal when he/she is accountable to one person. Think in terms of having three people with whom you can be completely open and accountable. Your sponsor or mentor can be one of your accountability partners, but keep in mind that the word "partner" usually describes more mutuality in the relationship than is typical with a mentor. Your spouse should *not* be an accountability partner.

Acting Out/Acting In

Acting out refers to the practice of engaging in sinful or dysfunctional behaviors. When we are talking about acting out in the context of sexual addiction, then, we are talking about engaging in sinful and dysfunctional sexual behaviors. *Acting in* refers to rigidly controlling sexual behaviors in an unhealthy and primarily external way. It often means that sex (or some other behavior) is being strictly avoided, but the person isn't growing emotionally and spiritually. "Acting in" within a marriage can look like an addict not being sexual with his spouse. The term is often used synonymously with "sexual anorexia." "Acting out" and "acting in" are really opposite ends of the same continuum. They both can be attempts to control painful memories or emotions.

Addiction

Historically, the word "addiction" has been controversial in the Christian community. Some fear that the concept of addiction removes personal responsibility for sinful behavior. Some believe those who call themselves addicts blame their personal decisions on an "addiction." All truly repentant and humble addicts, however, always accept personal responsibility for their actions.

The medical and psychological community has several universal criteria for determining if a substance or a behavior is an addiction:

1. **Use of the substance or behavior has become "unmanageable."** This means the addict has tried to stop over and over again, but can't. There is a history of failed attempts. Some clinicians believe there must be at least a two-year history of an unmanageable pattern for a person to be labeled an addict. The word "powerless" has also been used to describe this pattern. Sometimes addicts refer to themselves as "out of control." Even when an addict creates destructive consequences for himself by sinful behaviors, it's not enough to get him to stop.

2. **The addiction gets worse over time.** This means that more and more of the substance or behavior will be needed to achieve the same effect. An alcoholic knows, for example, that as he continues to drink, he'll need more and more alcohol to get "high" or drunk. Sex addicts know that they need more and more sexual activity to achieve the same "high" of the acting out experience. This escalation can take two forms. The most basic is that the addict does more and more of the same kind of behavior. (i.e. start at masturbating once a month and progress to masturbating once a day or more). For some addicts, progression means they'll need new kinds of acting

out experiences to achieve the same "high." It's important to remember that most addicts won't progress to illegal, highly dangerous, or sexually offending kinds of behaviors. Some do, but the majority do not. Sexual addicts may be able to stop their behaviors for periods of time, but until they find healing, will always return to them. Over time, a pattern of repeated failure will be evident.

3. **Tolerance is one reason for the factor of progression.** Medical science is discovering new things about the human brain that broaden our understanding of addictive behavior. The chemistry of the brain adjusts to whatever an addict puts into it. Over time the brain demands more to achieve the same effect. For alcoholics, the brain adjusts to the alcohol and requires more. Thinking about sex and engaging in sexual behavior requires that the brain produce brain chemistry to achieve sexual response. New research is finding that the sexual chemistry of the brain can also become tolerant, which means more and more thought or activity is necessary to have the same brain chemistry effects—the feelings of arousal, excitement, and pleasure. In many ways, sex addicts are drug addicts, because they become high on the drug produced in their own brain.

4. **Because of the brain chemistry involved, addicts use the thoughts and behaviors that produce the neurochemical highs to either raise or lower their mood.** We say then that addicts "medicate" their feelings. If an addict is depressed, lonely, or bored, he/she can think of exciting sexual encounters, either remembered or imagined, and the arousal part of the sexual response produces chemicals that raise his/her mood. If an addict is stressed, anxious, or fearful, he/she will tend to think of the relationship or romance quality of the encounter. These associated brain chemicals create a feeling of well-being and contentment that lowers his/her mood. Most addicts are capable of both kinds of thoughts, and therefore, can both raise and lower their moods depending on their feelings at the moment.

5. **Finally, addicts act out despite negative consequences.** Addicts don't pay attention to negative consequences and are in what's commonly called "denial." They also usually "minimize" or "rationalize" their acting out, despite the consequences. Until an addict decides to surrender control of fears that prevent him/her from getting help, the addict will continue to act out. Addicts may also continue to act out because it's usually a slow and insidious form of suicide. They know at some level they are destroying their lives, but their depression prevents them from caring.

Bottom Line

A "bottom line" is a boundary that refers to the distinction between which behaviors are tolerable and which ones are not. An addict may have a bottom line as to what sexual behaviors are outside of his definition of sobriety. A spouse may have one about which sexual behaviors would cause her to leave if they happened again. This kind of bottom line is sometimes referred to as "a line in the sand." Several Twelve Step fellowships refer to bottom lines as "inner circle" behaviors. The inner circle is the place that includes all the behaviors that are not allowed in the recovering addict's life. So, if an addict's bottom line dictates that no masturbation is allowed, he might also say that masturbation is in his inner circle.

Boundaries

In simplest terms, boundaries are guidelines for emotional and physical safety. They define which behaviors should and should not occur in relationships and in families. They proscribe what behaviors *should not* be allowed, and when these boundaries are violated, that is "invasion." Boundaries also prescribe what behaviors *should* happen. When these boundaries are violated (or not upheld), then "abandonment" happens. Some people have non-existent or "loose" boundaries, which frequently cause them to be harmed in some way. Other people have "rigid" boundaries and do not allow themselves to be loved or nurtured. Many people do not know how to establish their own boundaries. They might be codependent. Other people don't know how to observe boundaries. They might be perpetrators of harm or abuse. Stating your boundaries is a way of asking for safety, which is a different practice from making "demands." A demand is a request for more immediate action, which may have more to do with fear and anger than it does with personal safety.

Codependency/Co-Addiction

These terms are often used synonymously, but there are distinctions. The term "codependency" was first used in the Alcoholics Anonymous (AA) community to refer to anyone who was in relationship with an alcoholic. The assumption was that these individuals tolerated drinking, as evidenced by their remaining in the relationship. These individuals, then, were considered "dependent" on the alcoholic. Since the alcoholic is "dependent" on alcohol, these people are "codependent" on alcohol. Codependents (usually spouses) tolerate an alcoholic and his/her drinking behavior out of their fear of being alone. It is more important for the codependent to maintain the relationship than it is to confront drinking and the problems it creates. As understanding about addiction has broadened beyond alcoholism to sexual and other forms of compulsive behaviors, the term "codependent" has come to refer to anyone who tolerates problematic or addictive behavior.

From this basic definition, many have written about codependency, saying that codependents abandon their own needs and attend to the needs of the addict. They are more interested in maintaining the approval and presence of the addict than they are in speaking the truth. This objective causes them to ignore their own needs and wants and sacrifice themselves. This sacrifice is out of their fears, not out of their strengths.

Codependents often "enable" the addict by making excuses for him or her and generally looking the other way. They also perform many of the tasks that an addict should be responsible for, which lead many to term codependents "doers." Accordingly, all that codependents "do" may save addicts from consequences, which often earns codependents the title of "rescuers." Finally, since codependents *seem* selfless, some have called them (and they may see themselves as) "martyrs." Essentially, codependency is a fear and anxiety-based disorder in which the individual has an addiction to approval.

Co-addicts are people who are in primary relationship (such as marriage) with an addict. "Co-addict" defines a relationship between two people just as "aunt" and "niece" indicates a certain relationship. Co-addicts may or may not suffer from the symptoms of codependency. Some co-addicts may not be consciously aware of their partner's addiction. They may seem strong and self-assured, but this appearance, too, can be a disguise for insecurity.

Please be aware that any labels, such as codependency or co-addiction, are used only for the purpose of identifying problems that need to be healed. We should always seek to use these terms in love and not in judgment. Some primary partners (spouses) soundly reject these labels as humiliating. They might say, "It's his or her problem, not mine." These spouses could benefit from exploring why they choose to stay in the relationship.

Compartmentalizing

In James 4:8, the brother of Christ says that we can be "double-minded." This term means that various parts of our brain can be at war with each other, which is certainly true with addiction. Paul, in Romans 7, says that we don't always do what we want to do, and that we often do what we *don't* want to do. One reason for this failure can be due to our "compartmentalizing." We segregate off parts of ourselves and aren't "unified." Another word for this state is "dissociating," which is a clinical term for a defense mechanism that refers to trying not to think about (or even to be aware of) something that is painful. Addicts often compartmentalize their sinful behavior and then deny that it even exists in reality.

Cross Talk

This reference simply means talking back and forth during meetings—the process of giving feedback. Some groups have struggled with this concept because certain members may talk too long, give too much advice, be too angry or judgmental, or simply be rude. People are encouraged at meetings to be good listeners and not to be amateur counselors. Members should always seek to be loving in their feedback. The practice for L.I.F.E. Groups is to allow cross talk, because it provides essential support when done appropriately. See the Safety Guidelines for further information on how to give appropriate feedback.

Cruising

This term refers to any ritual behavior designed to find a partner to act out with sexually or relationally. Cruising rituals may include dress, appearance, facial expressions, flirting, "hanging out" in certain places, or any variety of behaviors designed to find or attract a partner.

Cycle

A cycle is a predictable pattern where one thought or behavior leads to others that eventually lead back to the original thought or emotion. The sexual addiction cycle is explained in Principle One, Lesson Two of the *L.I.F.E. Guide for Men* and the *L.I.F.E. Guide for Women.* The recovery cycle is described in Principle Six of those same *L.I.F.E. Guides.*

Denial

Simply put, denial is avoiding or "denying" reality. Fear of consequences, such as others' reactions or our own painful emotions, is the usual cause of avoiding the truth. Denial involves both direct lies and the avoidance of reality.

Entitlement

All addicts/co-addicts need to "excuse" their behaviors. They search for reasons why it's okay to act out or act in certain ways. One of the main excuses is called "entitlement," which means that the person feels they *deserve* to act out. Some addicts keep a balance sheet in their heads and feel that when they've done enough good behaviors, they're entitled to do some bad behaviors. Spouses of addicts may feel entitled as well (i.e. to spend money or rage or have an affair) because of the addict's behaviors. Those addicts/co-addicts who see themselves as martyrs, unjustly treated in life, may believe that it's only fair for them to get something for themselves. Anger and narcissism are usually behind the feeling of entitlement.

Family of Origin

Your family of origin generally refers to your immediate biological family: your parents and brothers and sisters. It can also mean any people who have lived with you under the same roof. Examples might include step-parents, uncles, aunts, grandparents, and cousins. "Family of origin" can also indicate others who lived with you, even if they were not biologically related to you.

Fantasy

Fantasy is thinking about anything in an imaginary way. Sexual fantasy is entertaining thoughts about imagined sex, either about past experiences or about "hoped for" experiences in the future. Jesus said that even though you may only be engaging in sexual fantasy, it is still adultery. (Matthew 5:28)

Grooming

Grooming behaviors are those which seem innocent but are intended to gain someone's trust and therefore to gain opportunity for making sexual advances. Both sexual perpetrators and sexual addicts sometimes engage in grooming potential victims or sexual partners.

Intimacy Disorder

Intimacy disorder results from the core beliefs, "I am a bad and worthless person," and "No one will like me as I am." These ideas are foundational to sex addicts and co-addicts. Those who suffer from either disorder believe that if they tell the truth or express their real emotions, other people won't like them or may even end up hating them and leaving. This fear often means that the people whom we are most afraid of losing, like our spouse, will be the one to whom we are less likely to tell the truth. Intimacy Disorder is a fear and anxiety based disorder: fear that someone will leave us, and the anxiety that we will be all alone.

Medicating/Pharmacological Management

Medicating refers to using a substance or behavior to alter mood. Some substances and behaviors can elevate "down" moods such as loneliness, depression, or boredom; and some can depress (or lower) moods like anxiety, fear, or stress. Medicating has been called "pharmacological management" in that the person manipulates his own mood, becoming like a pharmacist of his own brain.

Minimizing

Similar to denial (and really a form of it), minimizing literally means attempting to make smaller what is true. An addict may try to minimize how his destructive behaviors affect himself and others, while a co-addict may minimize how the addict's behaviors are affecting him and others.

Narcissism

This is a clinical term that is more commonly used to refer to self-centered behavior. Narcissus was a Greek figure who loved looking at his own reflection. "Narcissists" often congratulate themselves on their own accomplishments or give themselves a wide variety of compliments. They seem to be thinking only about themselves and not others. Their own agenda is the most important. Narcissists often seem very grandiose and self-confident or self-assured, but they really are not. Instead they are very insecure and concerned about others' approval. Usually, these people have been "narcissistically wounded"—that is, they have experienced traumas that have damaged their sense of belonging and of being worthy. Narcissists actually lack self-confidence and are trying to bolster themselves.

Neurochemical

All activities of the brain are facilitated by the interaction of chemicals in the brain. What is sometimes called the electrical activity of the brain is based on chemistry, or "neurochemistry." Scientists have identified hundreds of chemicals involved in the process of communication among brain cells. Some people are born with genetic predispositions to having problems with the proper balance of these chemicals. Addictive and dysfunctional behavior can also alter the normal state of brain chemistry. Psychiatry is the medical science that seeks to understand the right balance and prescribe medications to correct such disorders.

Objectification

This literally means to view someone who is fully human as an object rather than a person. Sexually, objectification means to see someone as only a physical body and not as a person with a mind and soul. Objectifying is de-humanizing. When an addict objectifies someone, it is easier to lust after that person as just a body to be desired and used for personal gratification. Sometimes spouses of addicts, after learning of their mate's struggle, begin objectifying people as well, only seeing body parts or body features that might be attractive to their husband or wife.

Rationalization

This is an excuse or justification. Rationalizations are used to try to explain why something was or was not done.

Relapse

A relapse is a series of slips that reflect the crossing of emotional, spiritual, and sexual boundaries. A relapse is an on-going violation of sobriety.

Rubber-Necking

This simply means turning your head to take in a sexual stimulus (usually another person) for a longer period of time.

Sexual Anorexia

Those who struggle with food anorexia inhibit their eating. Sexual anorexics avoid sex. Other clinical terms are "inhibited sexual desire" or "disorder of sexual desire." Painful memories (conscious or unconscious) shut down sexual desire or availability. Anorexia is often about anger and/or anxiety. Sex addicts can be sexual with others and anorexic with their spouses. In these cases, guilt, shame, anxiety, or a variety of other factors shut them down sexually within their marriages.

Shame

One of the core beliefs of sexual addicts is "I am a bad and worthless person," which is a shame-based conviction. Shame, though, is not inherently bad. There can be healthy shame, which we feel when we know we need God. Unhealthy shame occurs when a person's life experiences, like trauma, lead him to believe he doesn't deserve God's love.

Slip

A slip is a one-time violation of sobriety in any form. "Slip" is an acronym for "**S**hort **L**apse **I**n **P**rogress." A violation of sobriety remains a short lapse only if the person learns from it, repents, and grows in understanding as a result.

Sobriety

Most simply in terms of Christian morality, a state of sobriety exists when a person is not being sexual with self or anyone other than his spouse. Any sex outside of marriage is a violation of sobriety. *So also is any sexual behavior used to medicate negative emotions, whether within a marriage or not.* As Jesus said in Matthew 5, these violations can include thought-life or fantasy.

Sponsor

A sponsor is the person who is your main accountability partner. The qualities of a sponsor are described in Principle Four, Assignment Two. While you will need many people in your accountability group or support network, a person in the sponsor role will serve as a mentor in your life, helping you plan your overall healing journey and providing counseling and spiritual direction. The primary role of a sponsor is to help you see yourself and your progress clearly so that you can make necessary changes in your life and avoid pitfalls on the road ahead.

Trauma Bonding

This is one of the trauma reactions described in Principle One, Assignment Three of the *L.I.F.E. Guide for Men.* It is commonly used to refer to dysfunctional attachments and unhealthy relationships. To be trauma bonded means that two people are attracted to each other because of conscious and unconscious characteristics that remind them of earlier people in their lives who wounded them. The unconscious hope is that attaching to this kind of person will provide a new chance to heal the old wounds. Basically, the hope is that if you keep repeating old behaviors you will eventually get it right. Sometimes trauma bonding occurs when one person hopes this time to be more in control, to reverse the roles, or to be the one with the power.

Trigger

There are two basic kinds of triggers in our program. It is generally assumed that the word "trigger" refers to the stimulation of inappropriate sexual desire or action. Any stimulus that is seen, heard, felt, smelled, tasted, remembered, or fantasized about that creates sexual desire or action (even if only in the brain) is a *sexual trigger.* Any stimulus (in the variety of ways just described) that creates emotional or spiritual feelings of anxiety, fear, loneliness, boredom, depression, or anger is a *general trigger*. Often, general triggers are also referred to as "emotional triggers." General triggers become sexual triggers when sex is used to medicate the feeling that the general triggers create.

We are conscious of many possible sexual triggers, such as looking at pornography or an attractive person. Memories of past sexual experiences (sometimes referred to as *euphoric recall*) can trigger sexual thoughts. Music, such as a particular song, can have the same effect. Other triggers may be more unconscious. They can be based on life experiences that we don't always consciously remember. Certain words or actions, certain expressions or tones of voice, certain times of the year or events, certain music, and certain sexual behavior can all trigger emotions or reactions. One key to identifying a trigger is to discern if your emotional reaction seems out of proportion to the event that's taking place. When that happens, your unconscious memory may be taking you to old places in ways you don't always realize. Have you ever had someone say, "You're overreacting?" The reason behind your "over-reaction" is probably some unconscious trigger.

A Final Word on Words

Words are words. Definitions and understandings change over the years. It's never a good idea to argue about definitions. They aren't something to live or die for. Words are simply tools to help us communicate. If there is a disagreement about some term, come to a group consensus and move forward.

In addition to these terms that I've defined, your group may encounter many others that I haven't included. Please contact L.I.F.E. Ministries with terms you'd like to know about, have a good definition for, or simply think should be included in future editions of this *L.I.F.E. Guide.*

Appendix C

Dealing with Disclosure

Many of the frequently asked questions I receive as I work with spouses pertain to disclosure, so I want to address some of those here.

What is disclosure and how do we do it?

When we talk about **disclosure** in the context of sexual addiction what we are referring to is the *process in which a person struggling with sexual addiction tells others about his/her sexual behaviors.* Although there are many scenarios in which a person's sexual behaviors outside of the marriage might be discovered and confronted, we believe it is important to have a formal time of disclosure between addict and spouse that is planned and mediated in a safe place.

Guidelines for disclosure we generally suggest to couples in recovery are as follows:

1. The addict works with a counselor or mentor in his small group to create a timeline of all of his/her sexual behaviors beginning with childhood and ending with the present. (The timeline includes any sexual abuse, first sexual experiences, as well as acting out behaviors before and after marriage.)

2. When the struggler is confident that the timeline of sexual experiences/behaviors is complete, he/she and the counselor talk about what *needs* to be shared with the spouse, what *may* be shared with the spouse, and what details need to be avoided during disclosure.

3. A formal time of disclosure is planned with the spouse when the couple and the counselor/mentor can meet together in a safe place.

4. During the time of disclosure the addict discloses the extent of his/her sexual behaviors while the spouse listens.

5. After disclosure the spouse is allowed to respond and ask clarifying questions.

What do I need to know about my spouse's sexual behaviors?

What is shared during a time of formal disclosure is very important. There are some things that absolutely *must* be shared in order for healing to take place in the marriage. There are other things that *may* be shared if the struggler feels safe enough to do so. And there are details about sexual behaviors that should *not* be shared with a spouse. Let's talk about what these look like.

Examples of Sexual Behaviors that *Need* to be Disclosed:

- Use of pornography in any form—internet, magazines, videos, etc.
- Compulsive masturbation
- Sexual behaviors that involved other people—intercourse, oral sex, lap dances, etc.
- Types of sexual encounters—anonymous encounters, one-night stands, prostitutes, short or long-term affairs, massages, phone sex, cyber sex, etc.
- Names of affair partners that the spouse knows or is acquainted with—friend, co-worker, church member
- Any behaviors that facilitated sexual encounters—placing personal ads, chatting on-line, going to strip clubs or bars, etc.
- Any sexual behaviors that resulted in pregnancies, abortions, or children
- Any illegal sexual behaviors—voyeurism, exhibitionism, etc.
- Any financial and/or legal consequences of which a spouse is unaware
- Any physical consequences of which a spouse is unaware—contraction of an STD
- Sexual involvement with children or minors

Examples of Sexual Behaviors that *May* be Disclosed:

- Sexual abuse experienced as a child
- Sexual behaviors and encounters that happened before engagement/marriage

Examples of Details to *Avoid* During Disclosure:

- Specific websites addict frequented
- Specific times/places where sexual encounters occurred.
- Names of partners spouse does not know
- Details about the sexual encounter—what person was wearing, physical characteristics of the partner, what they did together, what they said, etc.

But I want to know everything. Why shouldn't I know all the details?

As a spouse I know how difficult it is when you first learn about your husband's/wife's betrayal. You want to make sense of it all, and a million questions swirl around in your head. I just want to tell you that knowing details about your spouse's sexual behaviors will end up hurting you. Details help us to picture or visualize our spouse doing or participating in sexual behaviors with others. The more details we know about our spouse's experiences, the harder it will be for us to let go of the hurt and pain and move through the grieving process. Details make things more real and more powerful. When we picture something in our minds, the emotional impact is much greater. So, please, take my advice. Do not seek to know details about all that your spouse has done. You will have enough to grieve as it is. And don't forget that you can talk to your small group about your fears and concerns. Those further along on the journey will be able to help you during this difficult time.

What questions should I ask?

There are some good questions to ask your spouse after he/she discloses. Let me share some examples of those kinds of questions with you.

- You can check out intuitions/suspicions you had at the time. (So, that night when I caught you on the computer at 2 a.m. you were looking at porn?)
- You can ask how the addiction has impacted your spouse's relationship with you. (Is this the reason we haven't had sex in three months?)
- You can ask about how the addiction has impacted your family's finances. (How much of our money have you spent acting out sexually?)
- You can ask about consequences of sexual behaviors that impact you. (Did you have unprotected sex?)
- You can address any fears you have related to your spouse's addiction. (Have you done anything inappropriate with our children? Did you ever leave our children alone or unsupervised when you were acting out?)
- You can ask about the length of affairs.

I would also encourage you to express how you are feeling about what you have learned as clearly as you can, using "*I feel...about...because*" statements. It will be very helpful for your spouse to hear from you how his/her behaviors have impacted you and the marriage. And you will benefit from being honest about what is going on inside of you as you begin the grieving process.

What if I think of other questions later?

Often during a time of disclosure you may be so overwhelmed by what you learn that you are too numb and confused to ask any questions. Later, usually a day or two after the disclosure session, all of those un-asked and un-answered questions come to your mind riding a huge wave of anger and anxiety. If and when you experience this tidal wave of fear and doubts and questions, I would encourage you to take some time to think about what you are feeling and thinking before you approach your spouse. On my own journey I have found it helpful to:

- Get away by myself to a place where I could focus and concentrate.
- Invite the Lord to join me in the painful process of fearing and doubting my spouse's integrity and love for me.
- Write down all of my questions.
- Read each question and ask myself, "Why do I want to know that?"
- Cross out questions that are asking for more details about things I already know.
- Put a star by questions that seem to be valid concerns and need to be addressed.
- Call my counselor and/or group members to ask for feedback on the questions I have marked with a star.
- If others agree that my questions are valid, plan a time with my spouse to discuss them. (You may need to set up another counseling appointment if you have a significant number of questions or if you feel you spouse has been dishonest in his/her initial disclosure.)

How can I be sure my spouse has told me everything?

The answer to this question falls somewhere between "you can't" and "you'll know." If your spouse is pursuing God and working diligently on his/her recovery, then over time your spouse will be completely honest with you and eventually disclose everything that you need to know. However, if your spouse is not pursuing recovery, he/she is probably not going to be honest with you about everything. In that case, God Himself will show you what you need to know.

Do I really believe that? Absolutely. In my own life and the lives of other spouses I have worked with, God has proved his faithfulness to reveal the truth time and time again. You don't have to be the private detective anymore, but it will take a commitment on your part to leave the investigative and uncovering work to God. That means you must be able to trust God with your spouse. If you are finding yourself consumed with fear and continually looking for evidence of your spouse's sexual behaviors, it might be that you have something in your heart that prevents you from trusting God. On my own journey I have found it very helpful to look at my past. Messages we carry from our pasts greatly influence our ability to trust.

I do want to mention here that there may be times that your spouse will need to disclose other pieces of information that he/she did not share initially. This "dribble" method of disclosure, as I like to call it, happens most often for one of four reasons. First, sexual sin causes a great deal of shame. Whatever behaviors a struggler seems as particularly shameful, he/she may have great difficulty sharing—even with a counselor. Second, your spouse may withhold some information at the time of disclosure if he feels that particular behaviors will result in losses he/she is not ready to face or experience. Third, because some of our spouses have engaged in so many sexual encounters with others, they may actually forget about experiences. Addicts can also have black-outs and not remember what they did during an addictive cycle. Finally, it's very difficult for addicts to witness the pain they've caused others. Sometimes, they just can't bear to see those they love hurt any more and so they omit certain facts during initial disclosure.

The good news is that if your spouse is pursuing healing and recovery, God is actively at work in his/her heart and life. Many times God will remind a struggler of sexual behaviors that he/she has forgotten to disclose or prompt him/her to do the pain and share information that he/she has deliberately withheld. As God works in your spouse's life all of the secrets are being exposed and his/her mind is being renewed and transformed.

The bad news is that we end up grieving all over again when our spouses disclose additional information about their sexual behaviors. If you end up experiencing the "dribble method" in your own marriage, remember that your spouse's choices are more about him/her than about you.

What do I tell my family and close friends?

As you think about disclosing to family and friends, you must determine how much they need to know about your spouse's struggles and behaviors. Most often family members only need to know generalities. Remember, details make the emotional impact of truth much greater. If a family member or friend asks for details, your response should be, "I'm not comfortable answering that question." Be as specific as you can to avoid confusion or unnecessary fears, but limit what you tell family members in order not to expose them to more than they might be able to handle. Keep in mind that you have a support group and probably a counselor to talk to. Most of your family members will have to deal with the bad news without that kind of support. Also when you talk to family members, remember to use language that they understand and try to express the behavior in a way that shows why it is so hurtful to you.

For example, in my situation instead of saying, "Troy is a sex addict," I would say something like, "Troy was unfaithful in our marriage with more than one woman, and I am really struggling with his betrayal." If your spouse is addicted to pornography you could say, "My husband has a problem with pornography that has impacted his ability to relate to me and our children."

Remember that some family members and friends are safer than others. Seek advice and counsel from those in your small group about when and what to share with those you love.

What about our children? What do I tell them?

We firmly believe that disclosing to children in progressive and age-appropriate ways is healing for the child and for the family as a whole. Children are very sensitive to tensions between parents. Often they will blame themselves for marital disagreements and discord. Talking about what they already know validates their feelings and helps them to feel connected to you—even if the information you share causes them pain. Preschoolers can understand that Daddy lied to Mommy and hurt her heart very much. Elementary children can grasp the fact that Mommy had a friendship with another person that she should have had only with Daddy. Teenagers can handle even more information, and adult children should be told the general facts of the situation.

In our home we live by the motto, "Secrecy kills but honesty heals." As our children grow, we will continue to share more and more of our story with them. We want them to see that God loves us when we behave badly, that there are consequences for our choices, and that God can redeem any situation we give to Him.

One more thing I would add, if your spouse is in recovery, the best possible way to disclose to your children is for you and your spouse to sit down together as your spouse shares what he/she has done and any consequences that will affect the family as a whole. Children need words of security. Don't lie in order to make them feel secure, but do reassure them about the things that won't change during the coming weeks and months. Also, remember to give your children a chance to share how they are feeling and express any fears they may have.

Whose responsibility is it to tell my spouse's parents about the problem?

Often when we find out about our spouse's sexual addiction, the first phone call we make is to our parents. Our spouses, however, may struggle with telling their parents about their problem. Facing the disappointment of parents is a huge hurdle to overcome. In our opinion, however, it is your spouse's responsibility to tell his/her parents—not yours. It's part of the hard work your spouse must do—facing his/her sin and taking responsibility for it. Don't rescue your spouse from that work.

If your spouse is blaming you for the problems in your marriage, it is still not your responsibility to tell your in-laws. You can say, "Your son/daughter is not being completely honest with you. The marriage has been damaged greatly by his/her choices. I'm really hurting right now, but it is his/her responsibility to be honest with you about what is going on." If your spouse's parents really care for you and are interested in knowing the truth, they will confront their child. If they are unhealthy and deceived, then they won't believe anything you tell them anyway.

Should my spouse meet with my parents for a time of reconciliation?

If your parents are aware of the problem, are safe people (i.e. won't meet him/her at the door with a shotgun), and are willing to talk with your spouse, I think it is a very good and Scriptural thing to do. Your family needs to know that your spouse is sorry for what he/she has done to you and to them. Regardless of how your family members respond, it is a great exercise in obedience and faith for your spouse. I would say, however, that a plan to meet your parents and apologize should be initiated by your spouse—not you. That's your spouse's stuff. Let God work in your spouse's heart to bring him/her to that place of maturity and obedience.

What should I do if my spouse doesn't want me to tell anyone about his/her struggle?

Especially in situations where the spouse is not working on recovery, this is a very common response. If this is your situation, you will need great discernment and great courage. Tell your spouse that you need a place to talk about how his/her sexual behaviors have impacted you. Assure your spouse that you will use discretion. Then find a counselor, become involved in a confidential support group, and if you have a safe friend or two, share with them as well. Be respectful. Talk to your spouse about the nature of what you are sharing and who you are talking with. But also be firm about getting your heart the help it needs.

Because you have been greatly impacted by your spouse's sinful choices, it is now your responsibility to make healthy choices and live in such a way that you can heal and grow. You can't heal apart from healthy relationships, so telling safe others is a necessary part of your recovery. You may need a lot of courage to stand by your word if your spouse threatens to leave you, but covering up your spouse's sexual sin in order to save the marriage won't work. You'll be miserable, and the marriage will eventually fall apart. So, be honest with safe people, be truthful with your spouse about who you are sharing with, and trust God to be at work in your spouse's life.

What should I tell acquaintances who are really not close friends?

Tell them the truth without sharing any details. Things like, "Yes, we are really struggling right now. I can't really share what's going on, but we are getting help. Please do pray for our marriage." Or you could try being very real. "Thanks for your concern. I really don't know you well enough to share details with you, but I appreciate your prayers for our marriage." Lots of truth. Healthy boundaries.

I'm too embarrassed to tell anyone about this. Do I have to?

Well, that depends on two things: Can you keep from telling others without being dishonest, and can you remain in relationships with others without telling? You have to have people, and you have to have truth. If the truth about your spouse's struggle causes you to isolate yourself from other people, you will never heal. Healing comes in relationship—and not just relationship, but intimate relationship. If you are lying about your situation, you will never heal—and neither will your spouse. It was secrets that got your spouse this far, and it is secrets that will keep your spouse (and you) bound. I can't make you tell safe people about your pain and your struggles, but overcoming your fears and your shame will be necessary for you and your spouse to continue on the journey.

What can I expect after disclosure?

After disclosure you will grieve. You will likely feel numb at first and then experience anger and sadness and despair. Your spouse may feel better than he/she has in years, now that all of the secrets are out. And you may resent your mate for being so happy when your world has been torn apart. Expect mood swings and tiredness. If you find yourself unable to sleep, eat, or function for 14 or more consecutive days, it is time to go see a doctor for help.

The most important thing you can do after disclosure is to be authentic with your spouse about what you are feeling and authentic with the friends God has placed in your life. As long as you are talking about what is going on in your heart—the good, the bad, and the ugly—you are on the healing journey. Withdrawing and isolating yourself will limit what God can do in your life to heal your wounds.

Appendix D

Printed Resources

A number of good resources are available to aid Christians in their journey of transformation. Through both printed material and the World Wide Web, those who seek to live in freedom everyday can find information and inspiration.

Because it is impossible to maintain an up-to-date list of resources in this printed L.I.F.E. Guide, visit these websites for current suggestions of where to turn for help in the areas of addiction, co-addiction, trauma, and recovery:

www.faithfulandtrueministries.com

www.freedomeveryday.org

www.hopequestgroup.org

For those spouses seeking to understand their mate's sexual addiction, we recommend the following books as core resources:

Mark Laaser. *Faithful and True: Sexual Integrity in a Fallen World,* Grand Rapids, MI: Zondervan Publishing House, 1996. ISBN 0-310-20836.

Marnie C. Ferree. *No Stones: Women Redeemed from Sexual Shame,* Fairfax, VA: Xulon Press, 2002. ISBN 1-591600-16-2.

Russell Willingham. *Breaking Free: Understanding Sexual Addiction and the Healing Power of Jesus,* Downers Grove, IL: Intervarsity Press, 1999. ISBN 0-8308-1791-3.

Ministry Resources

Faithful and True Ministries

Mission and Vision: The mission of Faithful and True Ministries is to provide resources to encourage sexual integrity to those struggling with sexual addiction. Largely through our own recoveries and through working with some of the finest minds in the secular and Christian communities, we have developed a program that restores lives, marriages, and families.

Services: A network of groups currently exists nationally. For more information, contact our partners at L.I.F.E. Ministries.

Ministry Leader: Mark Laaser, Ph.D.

Contact Information: Faithful and True Ministries
15798 Venture Ln.
Eden Prairie, MN 55344
Phone: 952-949-3478
www.faithfulandtrueministries.com

Walking Free Ministries

A Part of HopeQuest Ministry Group in partnership with First Baptist Church, Woodstock, GA

Mission and Vision: The vision of Walking Free Ministries is to lead individuals and families to walk in freedom from the grasp and effects of sexual brokenness. The mission of Walking Free Ministries is to do whatever it takes to expose the darkness of sexual brokenness, educate the Church about it, and encourage anyone in bondage to sexual addiction or codependency to encounter Christ and walk in freedom.

Services: Walking Free Ministries provides Christ-centered support groups for those seeking freedom from sexual addiction and for their spouses.

Ministry Leaders: Troy Haas, M.Div.
Melissa Haas

Contact Information: Walking Free Ministries—FBCW
11905 Hwy 92
Woodstock, GA 30188
Phone: 678-494-2668
walkingfree@fbcw.net

HopeQuest Ministry Group

<u>Mission and Vision</u>: HopeQuest is a group of ministries dedicated to helping people successfully overcome barriers to Christ-centered lives, marriages, and families.

<u>Services</u>: Support Groups, Discipleship Teaching, Successful Living Seminars, Mentoring, Counseling, Residential Program, City of Refuge Ministers Program, Retreats

<u>Ministry Leader</u>: Roy Blankenship
Troy Haas

<u>Contact Information</u>: HopeQuest Ministry Group
11905 Hwy 92
Woodstock, GA 30188
Phone: 678-494-2800
www.hopequestgroup.org

L.I.F.E. Ministries, International

-Living in Freedom Everyday-

<u>Mission</u>: The mission of L.I.F.E. Ministries, International is to encourage, empower, and equip God's people to live everyday in sexual integrity. L.I.F.E. Ministries works with church leadership to offer hurting people within local congregations a safe place to confront sexual addiction and brokenness and to walk in Christ's unconditional love.

<u>Services</u>: L.I.F.E. Ministries offers Christ-centered and relationally oriented support groups that incorporate spiritual discipline, small group accountability, and on-going prayer and support for those struggling with sexual brokenness. L.I.F.E. also provides recovery materials and training for support group leaders.

<u>Ministry Leaders</u>: Johna Hale, M.A.
Bob Hale

<u>Contact Information</u>: L.I.F.E. Ministries International
P.O. Box 952317
Lake Mary, FL 32795
Toll Free: 866-408-LIFE
Email: lifeorlando@yahoo.com
www.freedomeveryday.org

Endnotes

[1] Dr. Glen W. Davidson. *Understanding Mourning: A Guide to Those Who Grieve* (Minneapolis, MN: Augsburg Publishing House, 1984).
[2] Drs. Henry Cloud & John Townsend, *Boundaries* (Grand Rapids, MI: Zondervan, 1992), p. 29.
[3] Ibid, p.31.
[4] Claudia Black, Ph.D., *Anger Guide* (Mac Publishing, 1996.)
[5] *Webster's Ninth New Collegiate Dictionary* (Springfield, MA: Merriam-Webster, Inc., 1988).
[6] Dr. Patrick Carnes, *Out of the Shadows* (Center City, MN: Hazelden, 1992), p. 82-85.
[7]Larry Crabb, *Safest Place on Earth* (Nashville, TN: W Publishing Group, 1999), p. 91-92.
[8] Paul David Tripp, *Instruments in the Redeemer's Hands,* (Phillipsburg, NJ: P&R Publishing, 2002), p. 85-88.
[9] Dr. Mark Laaser. *Men Living in Freedom Everyday: A L.I.F.E.Guide,* (Fairfax, VA: Xulon Press, 2003), p. 105.
[10] Larry Crabb. *The Safest Place on Earth,* (Nashville, TN: W Publishing Group, 1999), p. 15.
[11] From the Group Guidelines of Love in Action Ministries, Memphis, Tennessee.
[12] Larry Crabb. *The Safest Place on Earth,* (Nashville, TN: W Publishing Group, 1999), p. 125.
[13] Paul David Tripp. *Instruments in the Redeemer's Hands,* (Phillipsburg, NJ: P&R Pub., 2002), p. 85-88.
[14] Story taken from John 11:1-44 (NASB)